REPRESENTATIVE AMERICAN SPEECHES

1974-1975

Edited by Waldo W. Braden
Boyd Professor of Speech
Louisiana State University

THE REFERENCE SHELF
Volume 47   Number 4

THE H. W. WILSON COMPANY   •   New York   •   1975

52395

THE REFERENCE SHELF

The books in this series contain reprints of articles, excerpts from books, and addresses on current issues and social trends in the United States and other countries. There are six separately bound numbers in each volume, all of which are generally published in the same calendar year. One number is a collection of recent speeches; each of the others is devoted to a single subject and gives background information and discussion from various points of view, concluding with a comprehensive bibliography. Books in the series may be purchased individually or on subscription.

REPRESENTATIVE AMERICAN SPEECHES: 1974-1975

Copyright © 1975

By The H. W. Wilson Company

International Standard Book Number 0-8242-0572-3

Library of Congress Catalog Card Number (38-27962)

PRINTED IN THE UNITED STATES OF AMERICA

PREFACE

AN OVERVIEW OF PUBLIC ADDRESS, 1974–1975

In the terms of the theatre, the period covered by this volume has been one of dramatic entrances and exits. Some of the exits were even shocking. Foremost, of course, was the resignation of President Richard M. Nixon and the inauguration of Gerald R. Ford. Those historic moments soon were followed by the collapse of US allies in Southeast Asia and the triumph of the North Vietnamese; the stir of presidential hopefuls eyeing the election of 1976; the continuing downward spiral of business activities; and, in general, the spread of cynicism among many Americans.

In the last two hundred years, few events—if any—have compared with the hearings of the Committee on the Judiciary of the House of Representatives that took place July 24 to July 30, 1974. The committee was considering whether to recommend the impeachment of Richard M. Nixon, the thirty-seventh President of the United States. The live radio and television coverage of the hearings brought the American citizen "closer than ever to the pulse of democracy" (*Christian Science Monitor,* July 24, 1974). At the conclusion of the hearings, the committee passed three articles of impeachment (by votes of 27 to 11, 28 to 10, and 21 to 17), but turned down two other articles.

In a sense, Gerald Ford operated in the shadow of Richard Nixon as Harry Truman operated in the shadow of Franklin Roosevelt. While Vice President, he attempted to bolster the Nixon Administration and became what one writer described as "an airborne circuit rider," traveling 110,000 miles, visiting 38 states, and making over 400 public appearances (Douglas E. Kneeland, New York *Times,* July 31, 1974).

His inauguration as President brought little letup in the itinerating of Gerald Ford. He has been away from Washington "almost as much of the time as was Mr. Nixon," wrote Joseph C. Harsch in *The Christian Science Monitor* (December 19, 1974). "He makes quick trips. Almost any day he is off somewhere to attend an anniversary, make a speech, wave at people." From August 1974 to May 1975 he delivered more than two hundred speeches; in one week in April he made seventeen major appearances. In fact, some persons have questioned whether he could carry on the rigors of his office and maintain his travel schedule.

The people of the nation have had many opportunities to hear and see the President in person and on television. He spoke about the economy on August 12, 1974, and called for "a global strategy for food and energy" before the United Nations General Assembly on September 19, 1974. On October 8, 1974, he presented his anti-inflation program to a joint session of Congress. And, hoping to bolster the sagging prospects of Republican Senators and Representatives, he campaigned with verve and energy—but to no avail. The Democrats increased their numbers in both houses as several incumbent Republicans went down to defeat. Continuing the Nixon foreign policy strategy, in November 1974 he visited Japan, South Korea, and the USSR.

Perhaps his most dramatic and, according to his aides, his most important, address thus far was his State of the World Address. It was over an hour long and delivered to a joint session of Congress and to the nation via the radio and television networks. Under the guiding hand of Secretary of State Henry Kissinger, he made a grave plea for military and humanitarian aid for the United States' beleaguered allies in Southeast Asia. Again he failed.

What image did the new President project? He was declared to be "basically a friendly, outgoing man" who suggests the "air of the all-American boy, well scrubbed, cleancut" and reminiscent of "his football and Navy flying days" (Vermont Royster, *Wall Street Journal,* August 9, 1974). Unfortunately, his ideas have not appeared to be either new, substantial, or inspirational. In spite of five speech writers (Bob Orben, Robert T. Hartmann, John A. Theis, John J.

Casserly, and Milton A. Friedman) who have worked on his pronouncements and even coached him on his delivery, President Ford has a pedestrian manner of speaking, referred to as "bland" and "flat," that tends to leave his audiences disappointed. As one writer said, "Usually, there is some strong applause in the first minute or two of a Ford speech, but then it tapers off until, toward the end, the audience sits in polite, rather sleepy, silence" (Philip Shabecoff, New York *Times,* October 29, 1974).

The fall congressional elections gave many examples of entrances and exits. The elections saw the defeat of several established officeholders and the entrance of several promising newcomers and significant challengers. The Democrats gained 43 seats and thereby captured two thirds of the seats in the House; they also won 3 seats in the Senate. In addition, they gained 4 governorships, including those in New York and California. Democratic candidates ran without opposition in 56 races, while only one Republican—Representative Charles W. Whalen, Jr., of Ohio—was so fortunate.

Perhaps the most hard-fought contests for the United States Senate were in New York between incumbent Republican Jacob Javits (the victor) and Ramsey Clark, a Democrat and former United States Attorney General; and in South Dakota between incumbent Democrat George McGovern and Republican Leo Thorsness, a former Vietnamese prisoner of war and Medal of Honor winner. In a state with one of the smallest populations in the country (about 666,000), McGovern spent $1,173,000 on his winning campaign. In campaign spending, in fact, he was exceeded only by Democrat Alan Cranston of California, who spent $1,336,000 (*U.S. News & World Report,* April 28, 1975). Two other dramatic victories in the Senate were those of Democrats John Glenn, the former astronaut, in Ohio; and of Gary Hart, campaign manager for George McGovern in 1972, in Colorado. In Arkansas, the Democratic senatorial primary provided a great surprise when Governor Dale Bumpers defeated incumbent J. William Fulbright, who had served in the Senate for five terms.

Four bitter struggles for governorships took place in California, New York, Massachusetts, and Ohio. In California, Democrat Edmund G. Brown, Jr., whose father was defeated in 1966 by Republican Ronald Reagan, defeated Houston I. Flournoy, a former college professor who had served as state controller under Reagan for eight years. In New York, Hugh Carey, a little known Democratic Representative, defeated Republican Governor Malcolm Wilson, successor to and choice of Nelson A. Rockefeller. Equally dramatic was Democrat Michael Dukakis' defeat of incumbent Republican Francis Sargent in Massachusetts. Former Governor James Rhodes (Republican), reversing the trend in Ohio, won a victory over a heavily favored opponent, John J. Gilligan, the incumbent.

Noteworthy, too, were the efforts of women in politics. The number of legislative seats held by women increased from 470 to more than 750, for a gain of 70 percent. Some of these new officeholders include Governor Ella T. Grasso of Connecticut; Lieutenant Governor Mary Anne Krupsak of New York; and Susie Sharp, chief justice of the North Carolina supreme court. Newcomers in the House include Martha Keys of Kansas, Gladys N. Spellman of Maryland, Virginia Smith of Nebraska, Marilyn Lloyd of Tennessee, and Helen S. Meyner and Millicent Fenwick of New Jersey. Throughout the year, moreover, women persisted in their efforts to push for ratification of the Equal Rights Amendment. To date, 34 states have voted for ratification; approval by 4 more states is needed for the amendment to become law.

With the exposure of illegal campaign contributions and the subsequent convictions or guilty pleas of businessmen for making contributions and of campaign aides for accepting them, the issue of campaign financing became a controversial one and was much in the news. Nevertheless, great amounts were still spent at all levels of public service. For example, in Louisiana, two opponents for the Public Service Commission each spent over $125,000. Common Cause, the citizens' lobby, revealed that by August 1974 the Democrats had raised over $22 million, compared to $16 million by the Republicans. Joining George McGovern of South Dakota and Alan Cranston of California as top fund raisers in the Senate were Thomas F. Eagleton of Missouri, Adlai E. Stevenson III of Illinois, Birch Bayh of Indiana, Jacob Javits of New York, Robert Dole of Kansas, and John Glenn of Ohio (New York *Times,* October 23, 1974).

Meanwhile, the 1976 presidential campaign has already begun. Gerald Ford has stated that he will run for reelection. Rumor persists that should he step down, Vice President Rockefeller would make a run for the presidency. To block this possibility, conservatives usually loyal to the Republican party have threatened to start a third party, with Ronald Reagan their top choice to head the ticket.

Among the Democrats there is a crowd of hopefuls. Senator Edward Kennedy of Massachusetts, though placing high on the opinion polls, declares he will not run. With sufficient strength and campaign financing to command respect, Alabama Governor George Wallace is making public appearances to demonstrate that in spite of his wheelchair he is able. At present he seems inclined to try for the Democratic nomination, but he hints that he could go the third-party route again. Senator Henry M. Jackson of Washington, well financed, has a substantial following. Old-timers Hubert Humphrey, Edmund S. Muskie, and George McGovern, in case of necessity, are ready. Representative Morris K. Udall of Arizona and Jimmy Carter started their campaigning in December. Carter, former governor of Georgia, has done considerable speaking throughout the South. Senator Lloyd M. Bentsen of Texas in the past year has traveled 200,000 miles in 36 states in a prepresidential canvass. Fred R. Harris, professed populist and former Senator of Oklahoma, has indicated that he will try again. Most commentators, however, suggest that no one in either party has demonstrated sufficient strength to excite American voters.

Yet, for those both in and out of politics, other avenues of opportunity do exist. Lecturing, for example, is still an excellent way to earn a substantial income. Among the three fourths of the Senators who augmented their annual salaries by lecturing were four whose extra earnings exceeded $40,000: Howard H. Baker, Jr. (Republican, Tennessee); William Proxmire (Democrat, Wisconsin); Mark O. Hatfield (Republican, Oregon); and Hubert Humphrey (Democrat, Minnesota) (*U.S. News & World Report,* June 2, 1975). In the wake of his Watergate-related conviction, John Dean III (who served a four-month prison term) nevertheless spoke at college campuses across the country for fees of $3,000 to $3,500 per lecture. After opening at the University of Virginia, he visited such colleges as the College of William and Mary, Georgetown University, Michigan State University, the University of Iowa, and finally Santa Ana College. He ended his tour two weeks ahead of schedule— perhaps because of harassment and embarrassment along the way. Others who gained fame or notoriety through Watergate accepted lecture engagements, including Bob Woodward and Carl Bernstein of the Washington *Post* (their reporting led to the various investigations), former Senator Sam J. Ervin (at fees of $2,500 per engagement), former Deputy Attorney General William Ruckelshaus, and the convicted Nixon aides Jeb Stuart Magruder and Egil Krogh, Jr.

Ronald Ziegler, Richard Nixon's press secretary, hoped to lecture, but encountered such a storm of opposition at Boston University and Michigan State University that he abandoned his tour. Murray State University of Kentucky paid former Army Lieutenant William Calley $2,000 to discuss his role in the My Lai massacre. H. R. Haldeman, the former White House aide who was convicted of Watergate-related crimes received a reported fee of $25,000 from CBS for a two-part television interview conducted by Mike Wallace. CBS had also previously paid the convicted Watergate conspirator G. Gordon Liddy for an interview. This "checkbook" journalism came under fire from the other networks and media. Editorializing on the subject of lecturing, *The Christian Science Monitor* (January 29, 1975) wrote:

It is an irony that many people deeply involved in or associated with the nation's worst scandal are now profiting from that involvement. . . . They are doing so by writing books, lecturing, and possibly even participating in movie making. . . . To encourage the Watergate figures to huckster their "ware" . . . raises moral questions. Surely inordinate payment to Richard Nixon, John Dean and H. R. Haldeman and others . . . adds to the cynicism and general disenchantment of the American people, who in some cases might feel that crime not only pays but pays well.

Groups, often in colleges and universities, seeking entertainment, stimulation, and enlightenment, have the opportunity to choose from hundreds of other personalities eager to sell their ware via lecturing. For example, the American Program Bureau, which boasts of being "the world's largest lecture bureau" (according to the *Guinness Book of World Records,* p 418) has under contract "525 persons of whom about 150 are active marketable speakers." Its catalog lists politicians, sports figures, entertainers, editors, authors, and radio personalities. Robert P. Walker, the president of the bureau, states that his top attractions are Dick Gregory, Julian Bond, Bob Woodward and Carl Bernstein, Ralph Nader, John Dean III, Nikki Giovanni, Frank Mankiewicz, and Louis Rukeyser. He says that Dick Gregory holds "the all-time record for college popularity," averaging 250 dates a year for the past ten years. How to classify this flood of oration is difficult. Much of it is little more than show business, although many lecturers, such as Ralph Nader and Julian Bond, have serious intentions.

An increasing awareness of the celebration of America's Bicentennial was already evident throughout the country. On September 5, 1974, the First Continental Congress (September 5—October 25, 1774) was recreated at Carpenters' Hall in Philadelphia. The event attracted political leaders from all of the original thirteen states, including all but two of the governors. Governor Mills E. Godwin, Jr., of Virginia was named president of the congress because Peyton Randolph, one of the original Virginia delegates in 1774, had been elected to the same post. Many speeches, including

one by President Ford, were delivered. Governor Godwin
concluded, "We have comported ourselves in a manner
faithful to our history" (New York *Times,* September 6,
1974).

On September 25, 1974, the House of Representatives
took a brief recess to observe and commemorate the meeting
of the First Continental Congress. Representative Barbara
Jordan (Democrat, Texas) read a portion of Thomas Jefferson's "A Summary View of the Rights of British America." Selected speakers for the occasion were Professor Ce-
cilia M. Kenyon of Smith College, Professor Merrill Jensen
of the University of Wisconsin, and journalist Alistair Cooke
(*Congressional Record,* September 25, 1974, p H9529–35).

At St. John's Church (a reconstruction) in Richmond,
Virginia, on March 23, 1975, Burt Edwards, a professional
actor, delivered Patrick Henry's "Give Me Liberty or Give
Me Death" speech in the manner that Henry had spoken in
1775. Also portrayed were other important colonial figures,
including George Washington, Thomas Jefferson, Richard
Henry Lee, and Benjamin Harrison. The following day the
speech was reenacted at the Richmond Coliseum before a
crowd of four thousand.

On April 16 and 17, the Massachusetts towns of Lexington and Concord braced for a reenactment of the famous battle that opened the American Revolution. This
historic area was invaded by thousands of tourists, dignitaries, Minute Men in colonial garb, reporters, television
crews, and demonstrators who sought to use the anniversary "to bring [the country] back" to what was "considered
its radical origins" (New York *Times,* April 17, 1975). On
April 18, President Ford formally opened the two-day celebration and spoke at the Old North Church in Boston,
arguing for renewal of America's "belief and commitment
to human rights and liberties." The next day he spoke at
Concord, receiving in the main an enthusiastic reception,
but he was booed and jeered by youthful protesters participating in the counterbicentennial celebration. He delivered a third speech at Lexington (New York *Times,*

April 20, 1975). The coming year will bring many attempts to memorialize our colonial and revolutionary times. We should anticipate numerous other pageants and renderings of colonial oratory and bombast.

In the past year or so the concept of freedom of speech has received injury on many college campuses. Radical groups have disrupted, harassed, and silenced speakers of whom they did not approve. Edward C. Banfield, the controversial but highly regarded urbanologist of the University of Pennsylvania, was prevented from speaking at the University of Chicago and the University of Toronto; professors have been harassed at Temple University, San Francisco State College, Wayne State University, the University of Connecticut, and the University of Washington. Perhaps the most tormented person was Professor William Shockley, the physicist who argues that blacks are inferior. He was confronted by hostile audiences at several colleges. In a somewhat different context, on September 9, 1974, Senator Edward Kennedy was refused the right to address a rally in Boston and was booed, jeered, taunted, and endangered by the throwing of eggs and tomatoes by opponents of school busing (New York *Times,* September 9, 1974).

After Shockley's appearance at Yale, a committee, headed by Professor C. Vann Woodward, was appointed to examine attitudes toward freedom of speech (Anthony Lewis, New York *Times,* January 26, 1975). One paragraph from the committee's report merits special attention:

The primary function of the university is to discover and disseminate knowledge by means of research and teaching. To fulfill this function a free interchange of ideas is necessary not only within its walls but with the world beyond as well. It follows that the university must do everything possible to ensure within it the fullest degree of intellectual freedom. . . . To curtail free expression strikes twice at intellectual freedom, for whoever deprives another of the right to state unpopular views deprives others of the right to listen to those views.

In the same vein, Supreme Court Justice Oliver Wendell Holmes in 1928 wrote that the principle of free thought implies "not free thought for those who agree with us but freedom for the thought that we hate."

A review of the rhetorical happenings of the year past leads this editor to observe that democratic decision making is never simple or easy. It demands intelligence, self-discipline, self-denial, and self-sacrifice. It finds its strength in the common bonds formed by humane individuals of enlightenment and civility. Democracy is based upon fragile tenets: recognition of the common dignity of all, good will and compassion, equal participation of all citizens, constant sharing of common counsel and insights, faith in group deliberation, respect for the minority, and willingness to abide by majority decisions. Supreme Court Justice Felix Frankfurter concluded, "The answer to the defects in our society is not denial of the democratic faith. The answer is more loyal practice of that faith."

These observations lead back to the opening theme of this essay. Developing national moods and attitudes, continuing international tensions, and the approaching 1976 presidential election portend still other entrances and exits —less traumatic and more promising, it is to be hoped, than those of the past year.

The speakers included in this compilation have been most generous in supplying texts, background information, and biographical data. I am also indebted to many persons who helped me in collecting and assembling the materials included in this book. Particularly helpful have been Clinton Bradford, Stephen Cooper, Francine Merritt, Harold Mixon, and Barbara Walsh. The members of Louisiana State University library staff have assisted me in many ways. Linda Rewarts, Janet Fahey, Holly McGowan, and Paula Richardson have contributed much by reading my difficult handwriting, taking my dictation, and typing the manuscript. To all of these persons and many others I say, "Thank you."

Baton Rouge, Louisiana   WALDO W. BRADEN
July 1975

CONTENTS

PREFACE: An Overview of Public Address, 1974–1975   3

IMPEACHMENT

Hearings on Articles of Impeachment by the Committee on the Judiciary of the House of Representatives   15

Barbara C. Jordan. An Introduction   19
Joshua Eilberg. For the Prosecution   25
Walter Flowers. Undecided   30
David W. Dennis. For the Defense   35

OUR LONG NATIONAL NIGHTMARE IS OVER

Richard M. Nixon. Speech of Resignation   43
Gerald R. Ford. First Presidential Address   50

POST-WATERGATE ASSESSMENT

William P. Rogers. A Brief Assessment of Where We
Stand Today   54

THE WORLD FOOD CRISIS

Henry A. Kissinger. Address Before the World Food
Conference   62
Earl L. Butz. Feast or Famine: The Key to Peace   81
Mark O. Hatfield. Global Interdependence: "Life, Liberty, and the Pursuit of Happiness" in Today's
World   89

THE PRESS: RIGHTS AND RESPONSIBILITIES

Potter Stewart. Or of the Press 97
J. William Fulbright. "The Neglect of the Song" 109

HIGHER EDUCATION

Robert M. Hutchins. All Our Institutions Are in Dis-
    array 117
James H. McBath. The Vital University 127

DEMOCRATIC LIVING: ASPIRATIONS AND ACHIEVEMENTS

Daniel James, Jr. "Given Time We'll Get It Together" 135
Yvonne B. Burke. "Aspirations . . . Unrequited" 143
Virginia Y. Trotter. A Shift in the Balance 148
John W. Gardner. People Power 158

THE BICENTENNIAL

Virginius Dabney. Facts and the Founding Fathers 168

APPENDIX: Biographical Notes 181
CUMULATIVE AUTHOR INDEX: 1970–1971 — 1974–1975 187

IMPEACHMENT

HEARINGS ON ARTICLES OF IMPEACHMENT BY THE COMMITTEE ON THE JUDICIARY OF THE HOUSE OF REPRESENTATIVES [1]

"Watching, one felt the uniqueness of America. Nothing like it could have happened in any other country," said Anthony Lewis, editorial writer for the New York *Times* (July 28, 1974), in describing the televised hearings of the Committee on the Judiciary of the House of Representatives, meeting to consider the impeachment of President Richard M. Nixon.

In opening the public hearings, Peter W. Rodino, Jr., the chairman (Democrat, New Jersey), gave the charge and the history of the investigation:

> This committee must now decide a question of the highest constitutional importance. For more than two years, there have been serious allegations, by people of good faith and sound intelligence that the President, Richard M. Nixon, has committed grave and systematic violations of the Constitution.
>
> Last October, in the belief that such violations had in fact occurred, a number of impeachment resolutions were introduced by members of the House and referred to our committee by the Speaker. On February 6, the House of Representatives, by a vote of 410 to 4, authorized and directed the Committee on the Judiciary to investigate whether sufficient grounds exist to impeach Richard M. Nixon, President of the United States. . . .
>
> The Judiciary Committee has for seven months investigated whether or not the President has seriously abused his power, in violation of that oath and the public trust embodied in it.
>
> We have investigated fully and completely what within our Constitution and traditions would be grounds for impeachment. For the past ten weeks, we have listened to the presentation of evidence in documentary form, to tape re-

[1] Held July 24 to July 30, 1974, Room 2141, Rayburn House Office Building, Washington, D.C. Speeches are taken from official publication, *Debate on Articles of Impeachment: Hearings of the Committee on the Judiciary, House of Representatives.* Ninety-third Congress, 2d session. U.S. Govt. Ptg. Office. Washington, D.C. 20401. '74.

cordings of nineteen presidential conversations, and to the testimony of nine witnesses called before the entire committee.

We have provided a fair opportunity for the President's counsel to present the President's views to the committee. We have taken care to preserve the integrity of the process in which we are engaged.

We have deliberated. We have been patient. We have been fair. Now, the American people, the House of Representatives, the Constitution and the whole Republic demand that we make up our minds.

Prior to the public hearings, the committee, meeting behind closed doors, had heard testimony and reports pulled together by a staff of 108 persons. When published, this material filled 8 volumes (4,133 pages) and included a summary of 306 pages.

As chairman, Peter Rodino, "the silvery haired, pebbly-voiced gentleman from Newark," maintained decorum, presiding with dignity and fairness. The 38 committee members (21 Democrats and 17 Republicans), coming from 21 states, pursued their difficult task with seriousness and thoughtfulness. Among the members were 3 blacks and 2 women. Six were under forty years old, 19 under fifty, and only 5 over sixty. All lawyers, they were characterized as "for the most part anonymous backbenchers, their names and faces scarcely recognized outside their home districts" (David E. Rosenbaum, New York *Times*, July 24, 1974) and as "competent, articulate, judicious" (*New Republic*, August 10 & 17, 1974, p 5). Oftentimes during the televised hearings it appeared they were speaking more to the viewers at home than to fellow members.

"The debate was alternately inspiring and wearying, grand and petty. After opening on a highly constitutional tone the committee shifted to the usual wrangling so often encountered in the legislative process. The real issues began appearing—issues of constitutional meaning, legal procedures, politics. . . . In the general debate the tone was mostly one of sadness in performing such a duty" (Anthony Lewis, New York *Times*, July 28, 1974).

Much of the time partisanship was not evident; both Democrats and Republicans voted for impeachment. The defense of President Nixon was carried by ten Republicans, the most effective of whom were Charles E. Wiggins of California, David W. Dennis of Indiana, and Charles

W. Sandman, Jr., of New Jersey (R. W. Apple, Jr., New York *Times,* July 30, 1974).

Each of the thirty-eight members was allowed fifteen minutes for an introductory statement. Reproduced here are four of the opening speeches made on July 26 and July 27, 1974, the first two days of the televised hearings. These speeches, not necessarily the most eloquent, represent three points of view: the prosecution, the undecided, and the defense. There is also an introductory statement. The editor has rearranged the sequence of presentation.

Barbara C. Jordan (Democrat, Texas), a freshman Representative, was known to favor impeachment. One of three blacks on the committee and one of the two women, she gained the respect of her colleagues for her poise and good judgment. When she was elected in 1972 the conservative Houston Chronicle praised her as "an eloquent spokesman—perhaps the most effective in the state's history against human injustice" (Jo Ann Levine, *Christian Science Monitor,* March 18, 1974). She has won many admirers in Washington and across the country.

With some emotion she expressed her stand: "My faith in the Constitution is whole, it is complete, it is total. I am not going to sit here and be an idle spectator to the diminution, the subversion, the destruction of the Constitution." In her statement here she sets forth the impeachment proceedings against the backdrop of history.

Joshua Eilberg (Democrat, Pennsylvania), a Nixon opponent, gives a cogent view of the case for the prosecution. He has been characterized as "a shy, balding, liberal career politician" (Des Moines *Register,* May 19, 1974). Eilberg stated his position clearly when he said: "The evidence is clear and overwhelming. Richard Nixon is guilty beyond any reasonable doubt . . ."

Walter Flowers (Democrat, Alabama), along with fellow committee members James Mann of South Carolina and Ray Thornton of Arkansas, has been called a typical New South politician. James R. Dickenson said that "they expressed their proimpeachment leanings in terms of moral outrage, patriotism, reverence for the Constitution and American tradition" (*National Observer,* August 3, 1974). *Newsweek* described these three southerners as "among the most eloquent speakers." During the hearings Flowers withheld a disclosure of how he would finally vote on the articles of impeachment.

In the statement included here, the Alabama Repre-

sentative represents the undecided portion of the committee. He finished preparing his statement only ten minutes
before his turn to speak (*Newsweek*, August 5, 1974, p 28).
He stated his position when he said: "I shall listen to these
debates, and only then shall I cast my vote. . . . And I can
only vote . . . based on the Constitution and on the evidence." Six short opening paragraphs from his statement
have been omitted.

David W. Dennis (Republican, Indiana) was one of
the most effective members for the defense. Recognized
as "the best lawyer" on the committee, Dennis was described as an "expert in fine points of law," who took "a
genuine intellectual delight in arcane legal lore," a man
"conservative in manner, conservative in ideology and
conservative in dress, in keeping with his district . . . the
model for . . . Middletown, USA" (R. W. Apple, Jr.,
New York *Times*, July 30, 1974). At tense moments he
became excited and let his anger show, yet was alert and
penetrating in his analysis and retorts.

Arguing like a lawyer, Dennis put the point at issue
as follows: "The question rather is whether or not proof
exists, convincing proof of adequate weight and evidentiary competence to establish that the President of the
United States has been guilty of high crimes and misdemeanors within the meaning of the Constitution." As a
politician, however, he included a powerful appeal for
expediency: "Our business . . . is basically legislative, and
not judicial, lacking as we do a clear and convincing legal
case, which all reasonable Americans must and will accept.
We would do better to retain the President, we in our
judgment elected to office, for the balance of his term, and
in the meantime place our energies and spend our time
on such pressing matters as a real campaign reform, a
sound financial policy."

AN INTRODUCTION

Barbara C. Jordan [2]

Mr. Chairman, I join . . . in thanking you for giving the junior members of this committee the glorious opportunity of sharing the pain of this inquiry. Mr. Chairman, you are a strong man and it has not been easy but we have tried as best we can to give you as much assistance as possible.

Earlier today we heard the beginning of the Preamble to the Constitution of the United States, "We, the people." It is a very eloquent beginning. But when that document was completed on the seventeenth of September in 1787 I was not included in that "We, the people." I felt somehow for many years that George Washington and Alexander Hamilton just left me out by mistake. But through the process of amendment, interpretation and court decision I have finally been included in "We, the people."

Today, I am an inquisitor, I believe hyperbole would not be fictional and would not overstate the solemnness that I feel right now. My faith in the Constitution is whole, it is complete, it is total. I am not going to sit here and be an idle spectator to the diminution, the subversion, the destruction of the Constitution.

"Who can so properly be the inquisitors for the nation as the representatives of the nation themselves?" (*Federalist,* number 65) The subject of its jurisdiction are those offenses which proceed from the misconduct of public men. That is what we are talking about. In other words, the jurisdiction comes from the abuse or violation of some public trust. It is wrong, I suggest, it is a misreading of the Constitution for any member here to assert that for a member to vote for an article of impeachment means that that member must be convinced that the President should be removed from office.

[2] For biographical note, see Appendix.

The Constitution doesn't say that. The powers relating to impeachment are an essential check in the hands of this body, the legislature, against and upon the encroachment of the Executive. In establishing the division between the two branches of the leislature, the House and the Senate, assigning to the one the right to accuse and to the other the right to judge, the framers of this Constitution were very astute. They did not make the accusers and the judges the same person.

We know the nature of impeachment. We have been talking about it awhile now. "It is chiefly designed for the President and his high ministers" to somehow be called into account. It is designed to "bridle" the Executive if he engages in excesses. "It is designed as a method of national inquest into the conduct of public men." (Hamilton, *Federalist*, number 65) The framers confined in the Congress the power if need be, to remove the President in order to strike a delicate balance between a President swollen with power and grown tyrannical; and preservation of the independence of the Executive. The nature of impeachment is a narrowly channeled exception to the separation of powers maxim, the federal convention of 1787 said that. It limited impeachment to high crimes and misdemeanors and discounted and opposed the term, "maladministration." "It is to be used only for great misdemeanors," so it was said in the North Carolina ratification convention. And in the Virginia ratification convention: "We do not trust our liberty to a particular branch. We need one branch to check the others."

The North Carolina ratification convention: "No one need be afraid that officers who commit oppression will pass with immunity."

"Prosecutions of impeachments will seldom fail to agitate the passions of the whole community," said Hamilton in the *Federalist Papers,* number 65. "And to divide it into parties more or less friendly or inimical to the accused." I do not mean political parties in that sense.

The drawing of political lines goes to the motivation behind impeachment; but impeachment must proceed within the confines of the constitutional term, "high crime and misdemeanors."

Of the impeachment process, it was Woodrow Wilson who said that "nothing short of the grossest offenses against the plain law of the land will suffice to give them speed and effectiveness. Indignation so great as to overgrow party interest may secure a conviction; but nothing else can."

Common sense would be revolted if we engaged upon this process for petty reasons. Congress has a lot to do. Appropriations, tax reform, health insurance, campaign finance reform, housing, environmental protection, energy sufficiency, mass transportation. Pettiness cannot be allowed to stand in the face of such overwhelming problems. So today we are not being petty. We are trying to be big because the task we have before us is a big one.

This morning in a discussion of the evidence we were told that the evidence which purports to support the allegations of misuse of the CIA by the President is thin. We are told that that evidence is insufficient. What that recital of the evidence this morning did not include is what the President did know on June 23, 1972. The President did know that it was Republican money, that it was money from the Committee for the Re-election of the President, which was found in the possession of one of the burglars arrested on June 17.

What the President did know on June 23 was the prior activities of E. Howard Hunt, which included his participation in the break-in of Daniel Ellsberg's psychiatrist, which included Howard Hunt's participation in the Dita Beard ITT affair, which included Howard Hunt's fabrication of cables designed to discredit the Kennedy Administration.

We were further cautioned today that perhaps these proceedings ought to be delayed because certainly there would be new evidence forthcoming from the President of the United States. There has not even been an obfuscated indication that this committee would receive any additional materials from the President. The committee subpoena is outstanding and if the President wants to supply that material, the committee sits here.

The fact is that on yesterday, the American people waited with great anxiety for eight hours, not knowing whether their President would obey an order of the Supreme Court of the United States.

At this point I would like to juxtapose a few of the impeachment criteria with some of the President's actions.

Impeachment criteria: James Madison, from the Virginia ratification convention. "If the President be connected in any suspicious manner with any person and there be grounds to believe that he will shelter him, he may be impeached."

We have heard time and time again that the evidence reflects payment to the defendants of money. The President had knowledge that these funds were being paid and that these were funds collected for the 1972 presidential campaign.

We know that the President met with Mr. Henry Petersen twenty-seven times to discuss matters related to Watergate and immediately thereafter met with the very persons who were implicated in the information Mr. Petersen was receiving and transmitting to the President. The words are, "If the President be connected in any suspicious manner with any person and there be grounds to believe that he will shelter that person, he may be impeached."

Justice Story: "Impeachment is intended for occasional and extraordinary cases where a superior power acting for the whole people is put into operation to protect their rights and rescue their liberties from violations."

We know about the Huston plan. We know about the break-in of the psychiatrist's office. We know that there was absolute complete direction in August 1971 when the President instructed Ehrlichman to "do whatever is necessary." This instruction led to a surreptitious entry into Dr. Fielding's office.

"Protect their rights." "Rescue their liberties from violation."

The South Carolina ratification convention impeachment criteria: Those are impeachable "who behave amiss or betray their public trust."

Beginning shortly after the Watergate break-in and continuing to the present time the President has engaged in a series of public statements and actions designed to thwart the lawful investigation by government prosecutors. Moreover, the President has made public announcements and assertions bearing on the Watergate case which the evidence will show he knew to be false.

These assertions, false assertions, impeachable, those who misbehave. Those who "behave amiss or betray their public trust."

James Madison again at the constitutional convention: "A President is impeachable if he attempts to subvert the Constitution."

The Constitution charges the President with the task of taking care that the laws be faithfully executed, and yet the President has counseled his aides to commit perjury, willfully disregarded the secrecy of grand jury proceedings, concealed surreptitious entry, attempted to compromise a federal judge while publicly displaying his cooperation with the processes of criminal justice.

"A President is impeachable if he attempts to subvert the Constitution."

If the impeachment provision in the Constitution of the United States will not reach the offenses charged here, then perhaps that eighteenth century Constitution should be abandoned to a twentieth century paper shredder. Has the President committed offenses and planned and directed and acquiesced in a course of conduct which the Constitution will not tolerate? That is the question. We know that. We know the question. We should now forthwith proceed to answer the question. It is reason, and not passion, which must guide our deliberations, guide our debate, and guide our decision.

FOR THE PROSECUTION

Joshua Eilberg [3]

Mr. Chairman, this committee and its staff have labored steadily for more than six months on the question of the possible impeachment of Richard M. Nixon.

During that time we have reviewed a huge amount of evidence, questioned witnesses, searched for precedents in previous impeachments, and for guidance from contemporary legal scholars, previous occupants of the Oval Office, and the authors of the Constitution. The evidence is clear and overwhelming.

Richard Nixon is guilty beyond any reasonable doubt of numerous acts of impeachable conduct, regardless of any standard we apply. He has violated his oath of office as set down in Article II, section 1, paragraph 7, to: "Preserve, protect, and defend the Constitution of the United States."

He has also violated Article II, section 3, to "take care that the laws be faithfully executed"; Article II, section 1, paragraph 6, that the President shall not receive, "any other emolument from the United States," other than the salary and expenses set by law, and, it is Article I, section 2, paragraph 5, which gives the House of Representatives, "the sole power of impeachment."

What we are faced with is a gross disregard for the Constitution and the very safeguards in it which the framers hoped would prevent the President from becoming a king or dictator.

The evidence presented during our hearings portrays a man who believes he is above the law and who is surrounded by advisers who believe they owe their allegiance to him and not to their country or the Constitution. For this reason they were only too willing to carry out his or-

[3] For biographical note, see Appendix.

ders and directions no matter what the cost to other individuals or groups or the nation.

As a result of this atmosphere in the White House, a conspiracy—which is still going on—was organized to obstruct justice. Every possible power of the presidency was used by Mr. Nixon to hide the fact of the existence of the so-called plumbers and their activities. He ordered his assistants to commit perjury and praised them when they did. He ordered every attempt to be made to frustrate the activities of the law enforcement agencies investigating the Watergate break-in.

Mr. Nixon tried to use his power as President to get the CIA to lie about its connection with the case. He also used his power to get the CIA to assist his gang of burglars in their illegal activities.

Perhaps the most horrendous of these acts was Mr. Nixon's permitting his candidate for Attorney General, the nation's chief law enforcement officer, to testify falsely at his own confirmation hearings before the Senate.

Mr. Nixon is also involved in three instances of bribery. He accepted funds through his political organization from the dairy industry in return for presidential favors. He ordered the payment of $75,000 to Howard Hunt to buy his silence on the activities of the plumbers. Finally, he attempted to influence Judge Byrne's rulings in the Ellsberg trial by offering him the directorship of the FBI.

Additionally, Mr. Nixon has ruled that he is a law unto himself by refusing to turn over to this committee all of the material it has either requested or demanded by subpoena. This decision by Mr. Nixon is an arrogant violation of the Constitution which places the sole power of impeachment in the House of Representatives. Nowhere else in the Constitution or in the thousands of laws passed by the Congress is there any limitation on this power.

Mr. Nixon's claim of executive privilege has no basis in law or historical precedent. No contemporary legal scholar has claimed that executive privilege can be applied in an impeachment investigation.

His own lawyer has filed no brief on this issue. He simply stated Mr. Nixon's claim in a letter to the committee, but he has never justified it with legal arguments or precedents.

As I stated before there is no historical basis for such a claim. In the one previous presidential impeachment there was total cooperation by the President and his aides. In fact, President Andrew Johnson even allowed the impeachment committee to look through his personal financial records and bank accounts.

In the past other Presidents have refused to give Congress information it has requested, but the record is clear and unanimous on impeachment. All previous Presidents have agreed that nothing can be withheld from an impeachment investigation.

President James Polk wrote:

It may be alleged that the power of impeachment belongs to the House of Representatives, and that, with a view to the exercise of this power, that House has the right to investigate the conduct of all public officers under the government.

This is cheerfully admitted.

In such a case the safety of the Republic would be the supreme law, and the power of the House in pursuit of this object would penetrate into the most secret recesses, of the executive departments.

It could command the attendance of any and every agent of the government, and compel them to produce all papers, public or private, official or unofficial, and to testify on oath to all facts within their knowledge.

When this attitude is compared to stonewalling, edited transcripts and notes, tape gaps, and executive privilege, it is clear that Mr. Nixon is not thinking along the same lines as his predecessors, who had nothing to hide.

Mr. Nixon has stated in effect, "You cannot do anything but impeach me, but I am not going to give you the evidence to help you decide whether or not I should be impeached."

If he is permitted to get away with this ridiculous and arrogant argument, the power of impeachment may just as well be cut out of the Constitution, for the House will have no power to enforce it, and the power of future Presidents will have no bounds.

Fortunately, the ruling yesterday of the Supreme Court has made it clear that Mr. Nixon does not have a power to withhold information on the absolute claim of executive privilege. If the President is required by law to turn over information he has refused to release under a claim of executive privilege for the criminal trial of Messrs. Mitchell and others, then certainly the demands of the grand inquest of the nation must be all powerful.

All of the offenses I have listed could come under the headings of bribery or high crimes. Where this leaves tax fraud and the pilfering of federal funds to turn Mr. Nixon's homes into palatial mansions I do not know, but I believe we must consider their effect on the nation.

Mr. Nixon's actions and attitudes and those of his subordinates have brought us to the verge of collapse as a nation of people who believe in its institutions and themselves. Our people have become cynical instead of skeptical. They are beginning to believe in greater numbers that one must look out only for himself and not worry about others.

At the same time we are becoming a people afraid to take a stand. Our citizens are afraid that if they take a position on a political issue their telephones will be tapped, their mail opened, and their tax returns audited as a means of punishment.

This result makes it imperative that Richard Nixon be impeached. It has been argued that Mr. Nixon should not be impeached, even if the evidence shows he is guilty if the national interest would not be served by his removal from office.

Mr. Chairman, it is my deep belief that not only is

Richard Nixon guilty of bribery, high crimes, and misdemeanors, but he must be impeached and convicted by the
Senate if we are to remain a free, courageous, and independent people.

UNDECIDED

Walter Flowers [4]

Now, to the problem at hand, and make no mistake, my friends, here and out there, it is a terrible problem. The alternatives are clear, to vote to impeach the President of the United States on one or more of the proposed articles of impeachment, or to vote against impeachment. And there is no good solution among these alternatives. We do not have a choice that to me represents anything desirable.

I wake up nights, at least on those nights I have been able to go to sleep lately, wondering if this could not be some sordid dream. Impeach the President of the United States. The Chief Executive of our country, our commander in chief in this cruel and volatile world that we live in in 1974.

The people that I represent, just as I do, and most Americans I think really want to support the President. Surely we want to support the Constitution and the best interests of the country. But, in so doing, we also hope that we can support the office of the presidency, and that citizen among us who occupies it at any given time.

But, unfortunately, this is no bad dream. It is the terrible truth that will be upon us here in this committee in the next few days.

And then there is the other side of the issue that I speak of. What if we failed to impeach? Do we ingrain forever in the very fabric of our Constitution a standard of conduct in our highest office that in the least is deplorable, and at worst impeachable? This is, indeed, a terrible choice we have to make. And as we on this committee suffer through these times, I cannot help but reflect on the words attributed to Teddy Roosevelt about the man in the arena whose face is marred with sweat, dust, and blood.

[4] For biographical note, see Appendix.

Now, some of the things that bothered me most are troubling to all people who fear that big government can encroach on the freedom of people. The institutions of this country have been set up by the people to serve them, to carry out those functions that are necessary to a peaceful and a free society. They are not created to serve the interests of one man or one group of men, or the political gain of anyone.

Such institutions as the FBI, the Department of Justice, the CIA and surely the Internal Revenue Service are given great power because the people, through Congress, have needed those institutions to guard and protect them and their liberty. Yet, there has been evidence before us that the White House had an organized effort to get the IRS to audit and harass enemies of the Administration.

The government in its role of tax collector must be above any political use. It cannot be an instrument of power, of punishment and of political advantage. The power of the IRS reaches into every life, and it is a chilling thought that it might be a political instrument to get the enemies of the government.

My friend, Tom Railsback, spoke of this last night, that to him as a Republican the use of the IRS to get your enemies is a frightening prospect, and in my state in 1970 we have evidence of the White House leaking tax information, contrary to law, in an apparent attempt to affect the governor's campaign that year. There has been evidence that the FBI, the nation's police, were used to spy on those who disagreed with the Administration, and then some evidence that the CIA was used to supply equipment and assistance to a sort of private police group to break into a doctor's office, and possibly to carry out other activities for some sort of political gain.

And even more troubling, there is evidence that when the Justice Department and the FBI sought to investigate the Watergate burglary and the Fielding break-in, the President and his associates systematically misled those agencies, withheld the truth from them, and furnished false proof.

And then most troubling to me, in the spring of 1973, Assistant Attorney General Petersen, who was really the acting Attorney General since Mr. Kleindienst had recused himself, met repeatedly with the President and told the President what the investigation had shown as to the involvement of Haldeman, Ehrlichman, Dean, and others. He urged the President to help in dealing with the investigation, and the President assured him that the information would be kept confidential. Yet, not only did the President relay this information to Haldeman and Ehrlichman, who were the ones under investigation, but helped them use it to structure a plan to defend themselves. And the President did not give Petersen the information that he himself already had. In fact, by Petersen's testimony, when he asked the President if he had information about the break-in, he was told "no," even though the President had been told the facts by Dean and Ehrlichman.

You know, the power of the presidency is a public trust, just like our office. And the people must be able to believe and rely on their President. Yet, there is some evidence before us that shows that the President has given solemn public assurances to the people involving the truth and the faith of his powerful office when those assurances were not true, but were designed to deceive the people and mislead the agencies of government who were investigating the charges against Mr. Nixon's men. If the trust of the people and in the word of the man, or men, or women, to whom they have given their highest honor, or any public trust is betrayed, if the people cannot know that their President is candid and truthful with them, then I say the very basis of our government is undermined.

And finally, Mr. Chairman, there is the problem of the basic relationship between the President and the Congress. This committee I think is struggling to act fairly to reach the truth, yet, when we have requested and subpoenaed certain evidence that we all felt, or most all of us felt was needed, it has been refused, or given to us in a form that perhaps we cannot rely on fully. But, you know, in our rush to recognize and identify all of these problems, which I insist that we must do, let us not forget here today, or any day during these proceedings that they exist for the most part because of what human beings did or failed to do in contradiction of their duties and responsibilities under our system.

Obviously America is a nation with many flaws, but it is also a nation with hope so vast that only the most foolish or the most pessimistic would fail to realize it. We have all made mistakes, and we will probably make some more in the future. Some of them have been big ones with important and even sometimes tragic consequences. But, my friends and fellow countrymen, we have not always failed, and it is important to be aware of our successes as well. In all of history there has been no other nation to do as much for our own people, while at the same time extending a helping hand of freedom and generosity and compassion to a world in need. And I say it is important to remember these accomplishments, and let us remember that some of them have been accomplished in the last six years under President Nixon, because they might otherwise be persuaded to abandon those values and those institutions that are responsible largely for these achievements and they are also, I say, our best hope for further progress.

Now, I have said on many times that we can make great progress and improve our society, and still not have anything that will live or last unless we concern ourselves with underlying values. If we believe in nothing, my friends, if we don't have a sense of moral purpose, then there is little possibility of our nation or we as individual citizens reaching the heights of which we are capable.

We have, in the tradition of this nation, a well-tested framework of values, liberty, justice, worth, and dignity of the individual, individual responsibility, and more. Our problem is not now to find better values, but I say our problem is to be faithful to those that we profess, and to make them live in modern times.

You know, I always think back to the Preamble of our Constitution. It starts off, as we all know, "We the people of the United States." And surely, at least to me, there is no more inspiring phrase than, "We the people of the United States." Not we the public officials of the United States, not we the certified experts, or we the educators, or we the educated, or we the grown-ups over twenty-one or twenty-five. Not we the privileged classes or whatever. But just simply we the people, we acting in our communities across the nation can pull our fragmented society together again. At the grass roots of our complex and mechanized and industrialized nation, we can renew the moral fiber of America. We, young and old alike, we can create an America in which men and women, and young people speak to one another once again in trust and mutual respect. We sharing common objectives and working toward common goals can bring our nation to a point of confidence and well-being. We can provide a soul and character so vitally needed in our native land.

You know, we are the people of the United States, and we can do these things. We here in this room are the representatives also of the people of the United States, and even more particularly in this case, the representatives of the representatives of the people. And we have an awesome task that no one else can do for us. Let me close my remarks here by paraphrasing something Harry Truman was supposed to have said once. "I try never to forget who I am, and where I come from and where I am going back to." And I would add that I cannot forget that I must get up every morning for the rest of my life and live with my decision here on these terrible alternatives. I shall listen to these debates, and only then shall I cast my vote. And I can only vote as I am convinced in my heart and mind, based on the Constitution and on the evidence.

FOR THE DEFENSE

David W. Dennis [5]

Mr. Chairman and my colleagues of the committee, all of us are agreed that this is the most important vote any one of us is likely to ever cast as a member of the Congress. Only a vote on a declaration of war I suppose might be considered as of equal gravity. All of us I think would like this vote to be right, to do right, and to be recorded as having been right in the long light of history.

This is an emotional matter we have before us, loaded with political overtones, and replete with both individual and national tragedy. Yes, I suggest that we will judge it best and most fairly if we approach it dispassionately and analyze it professionally as lawyers who are engaged in the preparation and in the assessment of a case. In doing this, of course, we cannot approach or decide this important matter on the basis of whether we like or dislike President Nixon, whether we do or do not in general support his policies. The question rather is whether or not proof exists, convincing proof of adequate weight and evidentiary competence to establish that the President of the United States has been guilty of high crimes and misdemeanors within the meaning of the Constitution so as to justify the radical action of his impeachment and removal and disgrace from the high office to which he was elected by the American people.

It is my understanding that the principal charges against the President with which we have to deal are divided into three general categories, and it is to these that I shall chiefly address my remarks in the brief time allotted. These general categories are first, the obstruction of justice and the so-called Watergate cover-up. Second, the alleged abuse

[5] For biographical note, see Appendix.

of executive power, and third, which may be included within the abuse of power category, the failure of the President to comply with the subpoenas of this committee.

It is my judgment that only the first of these categories, the so-called Watergate cover-up, presents us with any really serious problems for our decision. I shall, therefore, address myself to the second and third categories, alleged abuse of power and noncompliance with the subpoenas in the first instance and rather briefly, and shall use the balance of my time in a slightly more extensive analysis of the alleged Watergate cover-up, following thereafter with my conclusions as to the merits of the case.

Turning first to the matter of the failure to comply with the subpoenas of the Committee on the Judiciary, we have, of course, had a landmark decision of the Supreme Court of the United States just yesterday which has decided for the first time that a generalized and unlimited executive privilege cannot be exercised to override specific subpoenas issued by a special prosecuting attorney in the furtherance of a criminal case.

This decision does not bear directly on, nor, as a matter of fact of law does it enhance the power of this committee to issue subpoenas in these impeachment proceedings, because very unfortunately, as I believe, this committee has declined and refused to test and determine its constitutional powers in the courts of this country, despite the well-known statement of Chief Justice Marshall in *Marbury* against *Madison,* that it is emphatically the province and duty of the judicial department to say what the law is.

I believe, however, that the power of this committee in respect to the issuance of subpoenas is at least equal to and in all probability superior to the power of the special prosecutor. This decision, therefore, although we are not a party to the litigation, and derive no actual right therefrom, very well may, in my judgment in all probability will result in the furnishing to this committee of additional

relevant and highly material evidence which we do not
now have.

It is my judgment that should it appear that such evidence will be available to us within a reasonably short
period of time, then it will become our positive duty to
delay a final vote until we have examined this additional
evidence.

In assessing the President's past treatment of subpoenas
of this committee, however, we have no right whatever to
consider yesterday's decision of the Supreme Court, because
in addition to the fact that we are not a party to it this
decision had not been handed down when our subpoenas
were served. At that point the President simply asserted
what he stoutly claimed to be a constitutional right, and
which he is, in fact, still legally free to assert to be a constitutional right so far as this committee is concerned, and
we on the contrary assert a constitutional right in opposition to the presidential claim. Such a conflict is properly
one for resolution by the courts, and absent a binding and
definitive decision between the parties by the judicial
branch, it escapes me on what grounds it can properly be
asserted that a claim of constitutional right is in any sense
an abuse of power.

Turning to further alleged abuses of power, I look to
the proposed articles which we have before us. In proposed
article two, these abuses of power are alleged to be first
illegal surveillance. But, the seventeen wiretaps which are
chiefly complained of under this heading were all insti-
tuted before the *Keith* decision, and were not only pre-
sumptively legal at that time, but are probably legal in
large part today, since many if not all of them had international aspects, a situation in which the need for a court
order was specifically not passed upon in the *Keith* decision.

Second, use of the executive power to unlawfully establish a special investigating unit to engage in unlawful
covert activities. But, it was not unlawful so far as I am
advised to establish the plumbers unit, and I suggest that

proof is lacking that the President intended for it to engage in unlawful, covert activities.

And in like manner, it is certainly not established as a fact that the purpose of the Fielding burglary was, quoting the charge, "to obtain information to be used by Richard Nixon in public defamation of Daniel Ellsberg," nor is there any substantial evidence that the President knew of or authorized this break-in before it took place. In fact, when told by Dean about it on the morning of March 17, the President said, "What in the world—what in the name of God was Ehrlichman—this is the first I ever heard of this."

Third, alleged abuse of the IRS. Without going into detail, I suggest that the evidence here so far as the President is concerned is one of talk only and not of action, that the independent attempted actions of Dean, Haldeman, and Ehrlichman were unsuccessful and ineffective, and that the only direct evidence of an alleged presidential order in the *Wallace* case is a hearsay statement by Clark Mollenhoff that Mr. Haldeman said to him that the President requested him to obtain a report which, of course, is not competent proof of anything.

Turning to other alleged allegations of obstruction of justice, the first one we have in the proposed articles of specific action is implementing the President's alleged policy in the making false and misleading statements to lawfully authorized investigative officers. It would be interesting to have the authors of this allegation particularly plead and prove to whom and when the President was guilty of making such false statements, and it would be relevant to inquire whether these false statements, if any, were, in fact, made to an investigative officer when and while he was engaged in his investigative function.

If the President was guilty of counseling witnesses to give false statements, again, some specificity in pleading and proof are much to be desired. I do recall that he had everybody go up to the Senate and testify without immu-

nity, and that he counseled John Dean, not very effectively
it would appear, to always tell the truth, pointing out that
Alger Hiss would never had gone to jail if he had done so.

Whether the President had a design to interfere with or
obstruct the Watergate investigation conducted by the FBI
and by a phony attempt to enlist the possibility of CIA
involvement, or whether he genuinely believed, due to the
personnel concerned, the Mexican connection and other
circumstances that there might well be a CIA or a national
security involvement, appears to me to be a debatable
proposition, and in any case, the CIA disavowed involvement, and any delay caused by this episode was for a few
days only.

I predict that the allegations respecting the alleged corrupt offers or suggestions of executive clemency will on the
record of our hearings to date fall far short of proof. And
I believe that the testimony before us of Henry Petersen
himself very adequately answers the allegation of wrong-
fully disseminating information received from the Department of Justice to subjects of the investigation.

The matter of the payment to E. Howard Hunt of
$75,000, apparently on the evening of March 21, 1973, is
probably the most dangerous single incident insofar as the
President is concerned, because there is no doubt that in
the conversation of March 21 the President more than once
stated, and in dramatic fashion, that in order to buy time
in the short run, a payment to Hunt was apparently necessary. But, in the same conversation, the following exchange
took place. The President said: "In the end we are going
to be bled to death, and in the end it is going to come
out anyway. Then you get the worst of both worlds. We
are going to lose, and people are going to—" And Haldeman says, "And look like dopes."

And the President said, "And in effect look like a cover-
up, so that we can't do."

And John Dean told the Senators the money thing was
left hanging, nothing was resolved.

More importantly, the March 21 payment to Hunt was the last in a long series of such payments engineered by Mitchell, Haldeman, Dean and Kalmbach, and later on LaRue, and all so far as appears without the President's knowledge or complicity. And as to the payment of March 21, the evidence appears to establish that it was set up and arranged for by conversations between Dean and La-Rue, and LaRue and Mitchell before Dean talked to the President on the morning of March 21, so that even if the President was willing, and he ordered it as to which the proof falls far short, it would appear that this payment was in train and would have gone forward had Dean never talked to the President on March 21 at all.

And we need to remember in this connection that despite my repeated insistence and requests, this committee has never even bothered to call Howard Hunt, the chief figure in the alleged blackmail as a witness in the course of these proceedings, and where cover-up is concerned, we ought to remember that after all the President became fully aware and took charge on March 21, and surely he was entitled to a few days to check the facts. And that by April 30, Haldeman, Ehrlichman, Kleindienst and Dean had all left the government for good, and now are dealing as they should with the structures of the criminal law.

Time does not permit a further analysis of the evidence, but in conclusion I would like to leave with you a couple of thoughts. The first legal and finally a more general word.

First, if we bring this case and carry it through the House and into the Senate we will have to prove it. We will have to prove it by competent evidence. The managers on the part of the House will have to make the case. At that point, hearsay will not do, inference upon inference will not do. *Ex parte* affidavits will not do. Memoranda will not do. Prior recorded testimony and other legal proceedings to which the President was not a party will not serve. The witnesses never called in our investigation, and even never interviewed, will have to be called and will have to be relied upon. Someone will have to present this case in the cold light of a judicial day.

And unless a legally provable case is clearly there, we ought not to attempt it, we ought not to bring on this trauma, this injustice to the President, in fairness to ourselves and in consideration of the welfare of the country. Any prosecution is going to divide this country. It will tear asunder the Republican party for many years to come, and this is bad for the country which demands for its political health a strong two-party system. And impeachment is radical surgery on the tip of the cancer which needs therapy at the roots. I am as shocked as anyone by the misdeeds of Watergate. Richard Nixon has much to answer for, and he has even more to answer for to me as a conservative Republican than he does to my liberal friends on the other side of the aisle.

But, I join in no political lynching where hard proof fails as to this President or any other President. And I suggest this: What is needed is moral and political reform in America. The Nixon Administration is not the first to be guilty of shoddy practices, which . . . not established as ground for impeachment, are nonetheless inconsistent with the better spirit of America. Neither the catharsis of impeachment nor the trauma of political trial will cure this illness of spirit. We are all too likely to pass through this crisis and then forget reform for another twenty years.

Our business in the Congress is basically legislative, and not judicial, lacking as we do a clear and convincing legal case, which all reasonable Americans must and will accept. We would do better to retain the President, we in our judgment elected to office, for the balance of his term, and in the meantime place our energies and spend our time on such pressing matters as a real campaign reform, a sound financial policy to control inflation, energy and the environment, war and peace, honesty throughout government, and the personal and economic rights and liberties of the individual citizen as against private agglomerations of power in the monolithic state.

There will be another election in 1976, and we can enter our two hundredth year better by preserving our rights until that time, and not trying to purge our sins by the persecution of an imperfect President who probably represents us both in his strength and his weakness all too well.

OUR LONG NATIONAL NIGHTMARE IS OVER

SPEECH OF RESIGNATION [1]

RICHARD MILHOUS NIXON [2]

I have concluded that because of the Watergate matter I might not have the support of the Congress that I would consider necessary to . . . carry out the duties of this office in the way the interests of the nation will require.

Thus came to an end the stormy career of Richard M. Nixon, the thirty-seventh President of the United States. Via radio and television networks, at 9:00 P.M., August 8, 1974, the President, in his thirty-seventh presidential speech to the people, announced his intention to resign the following day.

The Watergate break-in and the ensuing revelations; attempts to delay and thwart ("stonewall") the various investigations; repeated denials of guilt; the hearings of the Senate Select Committee on Presidential Campaign Activities, lasting seventeen months and containing 2,250 pages of reports; and finally the House Judiciary Committee's nationally televised impeachment hearings, July 24–30, 1974, which ended with the committee's voting out three articles of impeachment—these were the events that led to Nixon's decision to resign.

Day by day, and month upon month, the net drew tighter and tension mounted. Each new development, more dramatic than the last, brought tragedy nearer. In the end, Nixon spoke to an anxious, confused, sad, but relieved nation.

The speech is not a great or memorable one. It is an important historic piece that attempts to recount the accomplishments of the Nixon presidency. But little of the old Nixon fight is left.

The following day, immediately before departing from the White House, Nixon delivered "a sorrowful goodby" to his staff and Cabinet in the East Room of the White House. Robert Boyd of the Miami *Herald* (August 10, 1974) thought that it was "a sentimental, occasionally moving performance. There was none of the bitterness or aggressiveness that marked his remarks in previous defeats."

[1] Delivered from the White House, Washington, D.C., August 8, 1974.
[2] For biographical note, see Appendix.

Declaring that "goodby" in English did not express his feelings, Nixon said he thought "the best is au revoir. We'll see you again."

The once imperial figure closed his political career as a broken man. James M. Perry of the *National Observer* (August 17, 1974) called the valedictory "strangely warm and touching." He continued, "Now he is gone. 'What's gone and what's past help,' it is said in *The Winter's Tale*, 'should be past grief.' . . . The king surely is dead, long live the king. Exit Nixon, enter Ford."

Good evening. This is the thirty-seventh time I have spoken to you from this office in which so many decisions have been made that shape the history of this nation.

Each time I have done so to discuss with you some matters that I believe affected the national interest. And all the decisions I have made in my public life I have always tried to do what was best for the nation.

Throughout the long and difficult period of Watergate, I have felt it was my duty to persevere; to make every possible effort to complete the term of office to which you elected me.

In the past few days, however, it has become evident to me that I no longer have a strong enough political base in the Congress to justify continuing that effort.

As long as there was such a base, I felt strongly that it was necessary to see the constitutional process through to its conclusion; that to do otherwise would be unfaithful to the spirit of that deliberately difficult process, and a dangerously destabilizing precedent for the future.

But with the disappearance of that base, I now believe that the constitutional purpose has been served. And there is no longer a need for the process to be prolonged.

I would have preferred to carry through to the finish whatever the personal agony it would have involved, and my family unanimously urged me to do so.

But the interests of the nation must always come before any personal considerations. From the discussions I have had with congressional and other leaders I have concluded that because of the Watergate matter I might not have the support of the Congress that I would consider necessary to back the very difficult decisions and carry out the duties of this office in the way the interests of the nation will require.

I have never been a quitter.

To leave office before my term is completed is opposed to every instinct in my body. But as President I must put the interests of America first.

America needs a full-time President and a full-time Congress, particularly at this time with problems we face at home and abroad.

To continue to fight through the months ahead for my personal vindication would almost totally absorb the time and attention of both the President and the Congress in a period when our entire focus should be on the great issues of peace abroad and prosperity without inflation at home.

Therefore, I shall resign the presidency effective at noon tomorrow.

Vice President Ford will be sworn in as President at that hour in this office.

As I recall the high hopes for America with which we began this second term, I feel a great sadness that I will not be here in this office working on your behalf to achieve those hopes in the next two and a half years.

But in turning over direction of the government to Vice President Ford I know, as I told the nation when I nominated him for that office ten months ago, that the leadership of America will be in good hands.

In passing this office to the Vice President I also do so with the profound sense of the weight of responsibility that will fall on his shoulders tomorrow, and therefore of the understanding, the patience, the cooperation he will need from all Americans.

As he assumes that responsibility he will deserve the help and the support of all of us. As we look to the future, the first essential is to begin healing the wounds of this nation. To put the bitterness and divisions of the recent past behind us and to rediscover those shared ideals that lie at the heart of our strength and unity as a great and as a free people.

By taking this action, I hope that I will have hastened the start of that process of healing which is so desperately needed in America.

I regret deeply any injuries that may have been done in the course of the events that led to this decision. I would say only that if some of my judgments were wrong —and some were wrong—they were made in what I believed at the time to be the best interests of the nation.

To those who have stood with me during these past difficult months, to my family, my friends, the many others who've joined in supporting my cause because they believed it was right, I will be eternally grateful for your support.

And to those who have not felt able to give me your support, let me say I leave with no bitterness toward those who have opposed me, because all of us in the final analysis have been concerned with the good of the country however our judgments might differ.

So let us all now join together in affirming that common commitment and in helping our new President succeed for the benefit of all Americans.

I shall leave this office with regret at not completing my term but with gratitude for the privilege of serving as your President for the past five and a half years.

These years have been a momentous time in the history of our nation and the world. They have been a time of achievement in which we can all be proud—achievements that represent the shared efforts of the Administration, the Congress and the people. But the challenges ahead are equally great.

And they, too, will require the support and the efforts of a Congress and the people, working in cooperation with the new Administration.

We have ended America's longest war. But in the work of securing a lasting peace in the world, the goals ahead are even more far-reaching and more difficult. We must complete a structure of peace, so that it will be said of this generation—our generation of Americans—by the people of all nations, not only that we ended one war but that we prevented future wars.

We have unlocked the doors that for a quarter of a century stood between the United States and the People's Republic of China. We must now insure that the one quarter of the world's people who live in the People's Republic of China will be and remain, not our enemies, but our friends.

In the Middle East, 100 million people in the Arab countries, many of whom have considered us their enemies for nearly twenty years, now look on us as their friends. We must continue to build on that friendship so that peace can settle at last over the Middle East and so that the cradle of civilization will not become its grave.

Together with the Soviet Union we have made the crucial breakthroughs that have begun the process of limiting nuclear arms. But, we must set as our goal, not just limiting, but reducing and finally destroying these terrible weapons so that they cannot destroy civilization.

And so that the threat of nuclear war will no longer hang over the world and the people, we have opened a new relation with the Soviet Union. We must continue to develop and expand that new relationship so that the two strongest nations of the world will live together in cooperation rather than confrontation.

Around the world—in Asia, in Africa, in Latin America, in the Middle East—there are millions of people who live in terrible poverty, even starvation. We must keep as our goal turning away from production for war and expanding production for peace so that people everywhere on this earth can at last look forward, in their children's time if not in our time, to having the necessities for a decent life.

Here in America we are fortunate that most of our people have not only the blessings of liberty but also the means to live full and good, and by the world's standards even abundant, lives.

We must press on, however, toward a goal not only of more and better jobs but of full opportunity for every man, and of what we are striving so hard right now to achieve—prosperity without inflation.

For more than a quarter of a century in public life, I have shared in the turbulent history of this evening.

I have fought for what I believe in. I have tried, to the best of my ability, to discharge those duties and meet those responsibilities that were entrusted to me.

Sometimes I have succeeded. And sometimes I have failed. But always I have taken heart from what Theodore Roosevelt said about the man in the arena whose face is marred by dust and sweat and blood, who strives valiantly, who errs and comes short again and again because there is not effort without error and shortcoming, but who does actually strive to do the deed, who knows the great devotion, who spends himself in a worthy cause, who at the best knows in the end the triumphs of high achievements and with the worst if he fails, at least fails while daring greatly.

I pledge to you tonight that as long as I have a breath of life in my body I shall continue in that spirit. I shall continue to work for the great causes to which I have been dedicated throughout my years as a congressman, a Senator, Vice President and President, the cause of peace—not just for America but among all nations—prosperity, justice and opportunity for all of our people.

There is one cause above all to which I have been devoted and to which I shall always be devoted for as long as I live.

When I first took the oath of office as President five and a half years ago, I made this sacred commitment; to consecrate my office, my energies and all the wisdom I can summon to the cause of peace among nations.

As a result of these efforts, I am confident that the world

is a safer place today, not only for the people of America but for the people of all nations, and that all of our children have a better chance than before of living in peace rather than dying in war.

This, more than anything, is what I hoped to achieve when I sought the presidency. This, more than anything, is what I hope will be my legacy to you, to our country, as I leave the presidency.

To have served in this office is to have felt a very personal sense of kinship with each and every American. In leaving it, I do so with this prayer: May God's grace be with you in all the days ahead.

FIRST PRESIDENTIAL ADDRESS [3]

GERALD R. FORD [4]

My fellow Americans, our long national nightmare is over. Our Constitution works. Our great Republic is a government of laws and not of men. Here, the people rule.

In these sentences Gerald Rudolph Ford, the thirty-eighth President of the United States, signaled the close of the months of anxiety, intrigue, charges, countercharges, revelations, and hearings. The Nixon Administration came to a close without a coup and confusion. The transfer of power was orderly. There was no hysteria among the citizenry. (See Bill Moyers, "No Coup . . . No Tanks . . . No Mobs," *Newsweek,* August 19, 1974, p 11.) With impeachment certain and conviction probable, President Nixon announced his intention to resign in a radio and television appearance August 8, 1974.

At the moment (11:35 A.M.) that Mr. Nixon's letter of resignation was handed to Secretary of State Henry Kissinger, Gerald R. Ford assumed the presidency, "under extraordinary circumstances never before experienced by Americans." At 12:03 P.M., August 9, 1974, Chief Justice Warren E. Burger administered the oath of office in the historic East Room of the White House. Before an audience of personal friends, Cabinet members, congressional leaders, and his family, Mr. Ford delivered a speech following the oath-taking ceremony. Marjorie Hunter (New York *Times,* August 10, 1974) reported that the President spoke "in his flat middle-western tone, but with what appeared to be a new sense of self-assurance."

Mr. Chief Justice, my dear friends, my fellow Americans. The oath that I have taken is the same oath that was taken by George Washington and by every President under the Constitution. But I assume the presidency under extraordinary circumstances never before experienced by Americans. This is an hour of history that troubles our minds and hurts our hearts.

[3] Delivered from the East Room of the White House, Washington, D.C., August 9, 1974.
[4] For biographical note, see Appendix.

Therefore, I feel it is my first duty to make an unprecedented compact with my countrymen. Not an inaugural address, not a fireside chat, not a campaign speech, just a little straight talk among friends. And I intend it to be the first of many.

I am acutely aware that you have not elected me as your President by your ballots. So I ask you to confirm me as your President with your prayers. And I hope that such prayers will also be the first of many.

If you have not chosen me by secret ballot, neither have I gained office by any secret promises. I have not campaigned either for the presidency or the vice presidency. I have not subscribed to any partisan platform. I am indebted to no man and only to one woman, my dear wife.

As I begin this very difficult job, I have not sought this enormous responsibility, but I will not shirk it. Those who nominated and confirmed me as Vice President were my friends and are my friends. They were of both parties, elected by all the people and acting under the Constitution in their name.

It is only fitting then that I should pledge to them and to you that I will be the President of all the people.

Thomas Jefferson said the people are the only sure reliance for the preservation of our liberty. And down the years, Abraham Lincoln renewed this American article of faith asking is there any better way for equal hopes in the world.

I intend on next Monday to request of the Speaker of the House of Representatives and the President Pro Tempore of the Senate the privilege of appearing before the Congress to share with my former colleagues and with you, the American people, my views on the priority business of the nation and to solicit your views and their views.

And may I say to the Speaker and the others, if I could meet with you right after this—these remarks—I would appreciate it.

Even this is late in an election year though there is no

way we can go forward except together and no way anybody can win except by serving the people's urgent needs.

We cannot stand still or slip backward. We must go forward now together.

To the peoples and the governments of all friendly nations and I hope that could encompass the whole world, I pledge an uninterrupted and sincere search for peace. America will remain strong and united.

But its strength will remain dedicated to the safety and sanity of the entire family of man as well as to our own precious freedom.

I believe that truth is the glue that holds governments together, not only our government but civilization itself. That bond, though strained, is unbroken at home and abroad.

In all my public and private acts as your President, I expect to follow my instincts of openness and candor with full confidence that honesty is always the best policy in the end.

My fellow Americans, our long national nightmare is over. Our Constitution works. Our great Republic is a government of laws and not of men. Here, the people rule.

But there is a higher power, by whatever name we honor Him, who ordains not only righteousness but love, not only justice but mercy.

As we bind up the internal wounds of Watergate, more painful and more poisonous than those of foreign wars, let us restore the golden rule to our political process, and let brotherly love purge our hearts of suspicion and of hate.

In the beginning, I asked you to pray for me. Before closing, I ask again your prayers—for Richard Nixon and for his family. May our former President, who brought peace to millions, find it for himself. May God bless and comfort his wonderful wife and daughters, whose love and loyalty will forever be a shining legacy to all who bear the lonely burdens of the White House.

I can only guess at those burdens, although I have witnessed at close hand the tragedies that befell three Presidents and the lesser trials of others.

With all the strength and all the good sense I have gained from life, with all the confidence my family, my friends and my dedicated staff impart to me, and with the good will of countless Americans I have encountered in recent visits to forty states, I now solemnly reaffirm my promise I made to you last December 6: to uphold the Constitution, to do what is right as God gives me to see the right, and to do the very best I can for America.

God helping me, I will not let you down.

Thank you.

POST-WATERGATE ASSESSMENT

A BRIEF ASSESSMENT OF WHERE
WE STAND TODAY [1]

WILLIAM P. ROGERS [2]

Approximately one month before William P. Rogers spoke to the annual Judicial Conference of the Second Judicial Circuit of the United States Court of Appeals at Buck Hill Falls, Pennsylvania, Richard M. Nixon, his close friend and longtime associate, had resigned from the presidency under the threat of conviction on three articles of impeachment. At this painful moment what would someone who had been so close to Nixon say? How would he assess the troubled events of the last two years? The lawyers and judges in Mr. Rogers' audience probably were curious about how this distinguished lawyer would react.

Not considered "a brilliant orator" (*Current Biography: September 1969*), Mr. Rogers nevertheless made a forceful presentation. Its importance lies in the fact that it shows that Rogers reacted like many other high officials and observers of the political scene. He readily accepted the actions of committees of the House and Senate in bringing about the downfall of the Nixon Administration.

On this occasion William P. Rogers, former Secretary of State under Nixon (1969–1973), was unemotional, judicious, and factual. He calmly recounted the forces that led to the resignation of his friend and former law partner. He said, "We are all familiar with, and shocked and chagrined by, the infamous role of several lawyers in the Watergate affair," but he expressed pride in other lawyers who brought about justice. His assessment of the public mood was most insightful.

In 1969 John W. Gardner, who was formerly Secretary of Commerce, made the following statement: "While each of us pursues his selfish interest and comforts himself by blaming others, the nation disintegrates. I use the phrase

---

[1] Delivered to the annual Judicial Conference of the Second Judicial Circuit of the United States Court of Appeals, Buck Hill Falls, Pennsylvania, September 7, 1974. Quoted by permission.

[2] For biographical note, see Appendix.

soberly: the nation disintegrates." This was a curious statement from a distinguished American. Such statements are
often excused as mere attention getters but they are disturbing and certainly are an affront to one's common sense. They
belong in the same class as silly statements about the dangers of fluoridation of water or expressed fears about the
end of the world. Our nation, of course, is not about to
disintegrate and it never has been about to disintegrate. On
the contrary, it is strong, healthy and respected. We are
concerned about and dealing with a number of problems as
one would expect in view of our nation's complexities, di-
versities and its position in the world.

In this rather upbeat spirit I would like to make a brief
assessment of where we stand today particularly in light of
recent events. It was just about a year ago that I left the
government service and for several months prior to that
time there was considerable comment to the effect:

(1) that the Executive was much too powerful—in fact
all powerful—so much so that the three coequal branches
of government concept was probably a thing of the past;

(2) that Congress was weak, ineffective and an appropriate subject for ridicule; and

(3) that the judiciary was ponderous, not relevant and
no longer needed to be taken into serious account in the
political equation.

Several months later, after Congress and the courts had
started to perform their constitutional duties as they saw
them this view changed. It was said by many then:

(1) that the executive branch had become weak, leader-
less and therefore unable to perform its duties;

(2) that Congress was faced with a difficult task of dealing with the crisis which, because of ineptness, it would
be totally unable to handle; and

(3) that the Supreme Court probably would divide along party lines and the country might well be faced with a frightening and paralyzing constitutional crisis.

During this period of time the legal profession came in for heavy attack because many of those who were involved in wrongful or illegal activity were lawyers by training, although I might add, only a few by profession.

Today, of course, the situation is completely changed again. Today:

(1) it is acknowledged that the executive branch performed its duties adequately during the crisis and that the new President has quickly and ably assumed the duties of his office and the members of the executive branch are capably exercising their constitutional role;

(2) Congress is being praised on all sides for the care that was used in the preparation of the material and for the effectiveness and fairness of its hearings; and

(3) the courts are being universally commended—and most deservedly so—for performing their judicial duties impartially and impressively with dedication and devotion to the Constitution.

During this entire period of time, of course, the news media played an important and necessary role in informing the public of the facts and commenting thereon. It may well be that the media can be criticized for the nature and scope of some of its comments, as some argue, but there can be no denial that the press performed impressively in seeking out the facts and in informing the American people of the facts as they developed.

How does Watergate relate to our profession? We are all familiar with, and shocked and chagrined by, the infamous role of several lawyers in the Watergate affair. We also take some pride in the role of many others; for example the members of the House and Senate committees (all of whom were lawyers), Judge Sirica, Attorney General Richardson,

Deputy Attorney General Ruckelshaus, and the Supreme Court of the United States. No useful purpose would be served in spending time trying to decide how the scales balance. Rather the emphasis should be elsewhere. We all recognize the difficult constitutional challenge our nation has had to face. We saw that the people of our nation responded to this challenge magnificently—with common sense and determination. We know that this would not have been possible were it not for the basic validity and vitality of our system of government. Thus our emphasis should be on the basic soundness of that system. It is a system respectful of men but devoted to law. It is a system which puts its faith in its people and at the same time expects the people to put their faith in the law. Throughout our history, this system has worked well and these last two years have underscored its soundness.

Tonight—and in the years ahead—our profession should take renewed pride in the morality and strength of the Constitution and laws that govern our nation. And lawyers, consequently, should have a reawakened sense of responsibility to maintain the highest standards of integrity and decency.

There is a recent book on the life of John Marshall, written by Leonard Baker, in which he says: "The story of John Marshall is the story of one man's devotion to law and his efforts to persuade his country of the wisdom of such devotion." Probably no man in our history would be entitled to take more satisfaction from recent events than John Marshall: John Marshall who successfully fought for the independence of the judiciary, for the power of judicial review which made the Supreme Court the final arbiter of the law and for the supremacy of the law over all men, including the President of the United States.

When have the three coequal branches of government asserted their authority more dramatically? When has there been less doubt about the independence of the judicial branch of our government or more confidence in its integrity? When has the supremacy of law over all men in our country been more graphically proved?

I mentioned a moment ago the effectiveness of public opinion in the Watergate matter. It seemed to me that the public responded to the evidence as it was disclosed with sophistication. It was not overly influenced by columns or commentaries. To an amazing degree it accurately kept pace with the evidence and the weight of the evidence. If this analysis is correct, and I believe it is, it suggests that the public is entitled to great credit in insisting that the facts be disclosed and in weighing those facts as the disclosures were made. It is noteworthy that as they were disclosed, partisanship became less and less apparent and the spirit of impartiality and objectivity that motivates most juries came into play.

The other remarkable fact about public reaction was its balance and patience. The American people were embarrassed, astounded and dismayed but they were never frightened or frenetic. Although it was a situation that our nation had never faced before, the public correctly concluded that the constitutional system would operate satisfactorily and should run its course whatever the cost. At a time when there were so many disparate voices in our country and so many bitter conflicts among people and institutions the American people had full faith in the system. In fact at times one got the impression that the public had more confidence in Washington than Washington had in itself.

What has been the effect of Watergate? On balance I believe our nation has been strengthened and that history will so record it.

First, it established that the impeachment process is effective in carrying out the intentions of the Founding Fathers as expressed in the Constitution.

Second, it established that regardless of the size of the vote in a presidential election or the success of the President himself—and it is generally acknowledged that President Nixon had an outstanding record particularly in the field of foreign affairs—that no President however powerful or however successful is immune from this constitutional process. Until this time there has been a reasonable doubt about whether the impeachment process had practical application.

Third, it underscored, as has happened on other occasions throughout our history, that the independence of the federal judiciary, made possible in part by the constitutional provision for life tenure of its members, is fundamental to our constitutional system of government.

Fourth, it established that Congress is qualified and able to play its proper role in the impeachment process and that the process itself is adaptable enough to meet any situation which might arise in the future. Parenthetically, I have no fear, as some have suggested, that the process will be misused in the future. Exploiting the impeachment process for partisan purposes I do not believe can be successfully accomplished and if attempted would be counterproductive. Certainly recent events raise no fears in this connection.

Fifth, it shows that the Twenty-fifth Amendment to the Constitution is of vital importance in our system and was enacted none too soon.

For the last twenty-five years, I have divided my time between New York and Washington. During those years I have been involved either directly or indirectly in four major upheavals which caused tremendous unrest and public concern in the nation. In each instance the intensity of this concern, I believe, resulted from the same or similar reasons. In each instance deceit, dissembling or a lack of candor on the part of national leaders was the cause or at least a major factor in creating a bitterness and divisiveness of major proportions.

The first was the McCarthy era. I knew Senator McCarthy well and was counsel for the Senate investigating committee on which he served. During the Eisenhower Administration I had a considerable amount of official contact with him when he was at his worst. He started out recklessly, making serious charges against many persons; then he dissembled and finally to cover himself, he lied and lied. When the public learned that he was totally lacking in integrity—after the congressional hearings (the so-called Army-Mc-Carthy hearings) had revealed the truth—McCarthy was destroyed and finished as a national figure. Fortunately the methods and techniques which he used in labeling all who opposed him as Communists and dupes of communism went out of favor and have not been tried since.

The second was the civil rights movement which reached its peak of intensity in the sixties and resulted in violence and bloodshed. Here again, I believe, the crisis was intensified by deceit. Over a period of years many of our national leaders—in fact our government—had lived a lie. It was claimed there was equal treatment under law for all our citizens, knowing full well the truth about blacks. The violence that occurred in the civil rights movement has subsided to a large extent, I believe, because there has been a recognition of the integrity of the nation's effort to put our Constitution's guarantees into practice.

The third period to which I refer, of course, was that of the Vietnam war. There were many reasons for the opposition to the war and all it involved. However, I believe that the intensity of the opposition—the deep revulsion on the part of so many—at least in part resulted from the deceit that led to our involvement. As we all remember the President promised that no American boy would ever fight on Asian soil and that we would send no ground troops to Vietnam. Our nation had to live with that misrepresentation and subsequent dissembling during all those years of that tragic war.

And the fourth period is Watergate—to which I have referred.

We learned from the McCarthy era that the public cannot be duped for any extended period of time by the lies of demagogues no matter how the lies are packaged. In fact, I think that era made our new relationships with the Soviet Union and the People's Republic of China much easier to achieve because the techniques used by McCarthy were so totally discredited.

As a result of the civil rights crisis we got the last constitutional skeleton out of the closet and properly buried it. And our nation has been strengthened as a result.

The Vietnam war provided a lesson, hopefully for all time that, if a leader in the United States wants public support in a crisis he must be completely honest and forthright with Congress and the American people.

And, as I have said, under the most trying conditions Watergate graphically demonstrated our dedication to the Constitution and the laws of our country—no matter who is involved or what it may cost.

Returning now to where I started: Our nation is not disintegrating—it is developing and progressing. It is not complacent and self-satisfied—it is still young and self-critical. We rarely get much satisfaction in solving problems because we are so busy searching out and confronting new problems. Our success in every field—science, technology, education, health, production of food, housing, transportation, communication, space, etc. astounds people everywhere. The initiative and drive of this nation are the envy of the world. We are the strongest, most prosperous and successful nation the world has ever known—I am proud of our country and confident of its future.

I rarely express such views because it is not necessary and because it sounds so blatantly immodest for an American to say. But occasionally—why not? After the last year and a half it seems to me that this is the occasion—and anyway it makes me feel a lot better to say it.

THE WORLD FOOD CRISIS

ADDRESS BEFORE THE WORLD FOOD
CONFERENCE [1]

HENRY A. KISSINGER [2]

At the opening of the United Nations World Food Conference in Rome, November 5, 1974, it was recognized that 460 million people in the world faced starvation; predictions were made that 10 million, mostly children under the age of five, would die from lack of food. Floods, droughts, and storms had destroyed crops in India, Africa, the Soviet Union, China, and the United States. The energy crisis resulted in higher prices for fertilizer and higher costs in planting, harvesting, and transporting grain. These factors plus the rapidly increasing world population (reportedly at the rate of 93 million per year), suggested that the need for a long-term solution was mandatory (*Newsweek,* November 11, 1974, p 56–8). Accurately, Henry Kissinger stated that what faced the nations was "a global problem requiring global solutions."

The World Food Conference, held in Rome from November 5 to November 16, 1974, grew out of a proposal made by Secretary of State Kissinger on September 24, 1973, in his first speech before the twenty-eighth United Nations General Assembly. On that occasion he said:

> The growing threat to the world's food supply deserves the urgent attention of this Assembly. Since 1969, global consumption of cereals has risen more rapidly than production; stocks are at the lowest levels in years. We now face the prospect that—even with bumper crops—the world may not rebuild its seriously depleted reserves in this decade.
>
> No one country can cope with this problem. The United States therefore proposes:
>
> > That a World Food Conference be organized under United Nations auspices in 1974 to discuss ways to maintain adequate food supplies, and to harness the efforts of all nations to meet the hunger and malnutrition resulting from natural disasters.

[1] Delivered at the United Nations World Food Conference, Palazzo dei Congressi, Rome, November 5, 1974. Quoted by permission.

[2] For biographical note, see Appendix.

>That nations in a position to do so offer technical assistance in the conservation of food. The United States is ready to join with others in providing such assistance.

On November 5, 1974, the Secretary of State gave the keynote address to the 1,250 delegates representing 130 countries and 165 delegations from 47 United Nations agencies assembled at the Palazzo dei Congressi in Rome. He spoke "in a slow, grave, measured voice in a city whose walls are daubed with hate slogans directed against him—signed with a hammer and sickle" (Richard L. Strout, *Christian Science Monitor*, March 3, 1975).

The speech was organized around a problem-solution development, giving a comprehensive view of what the world faces and what should be done. It is a plea for worldwide cooperation to meet the food shortages. His conclusion is particularly noteworthy. He said:

>Nothing more overwhelms the human spirit, or mocks our values and our dreams, than the desperate struggle for sustenance. No tragedy is more wounding than the look of despair in the eyes of a starving child.
>
>Once famine was considered part of the normal cycle of man's existence, a local or at worst a national tragedy. Now our consciousness is global. Our achievements, our expectations, and our moral convictions have made this issue into a universal political concern.
>
>The profound promise of our era is that for the first time we may have the technical capacity to free mankind from the scourge of hunger. Therefore, today we must proclaim a bold objective—that within a decade no child will go to bed hungry, that no family will fear for its next day's bread, and that no human being's future and capacities will be stunted by malnutrition.

These words were actually incorporated into the first resolution of the conference.

Any pronouncement by Kissinger is taken as an important policy statement and is carefully studied by foreign offices across the world. It is safe to say that this speech is probably the result of the creative efforts of the best informed men in the Department of State. It, of course, conforms to policies favored by the Secretary of State. But to assume that Henry Kissinger, who made "whirlwind travels to more than a dozen nations in October and November" (*U.S. News & World Report*, November 11, 1974), had written the speech in toto, would indeed be naive.

However, this fact of the jet age takes little away from Henry

Kissinger as an effective public communicator. Howard K. Smith, in an ABC documentary titled "Kissinger: Action Biography," suggested that Kissinger "will eventually be included among the dozen or so secretaries of state in history who have made some 'outstanding contributions to keep the untidy gain of nations in constructive check' " (Arthur Unger, *Christian Science Monitor*, June 14, 1974).

We meet to address man's most fundamental need. The threat of famine, the fact of hunger have haunted men and nations throughout history. Our presence here is recognition that this eternal problem has now taken on unprecedented scale and urgency and that it can only be dealt with by concerted worldwide action.

Our challenge goes far deeper than one area of human endeavor or one international conference. We are faced not just with the problem of food but with the accelerating momentum of our interdependence. The world is midway between the end of the Second World War and the beginning of the twenty-first century. We are stranded between old conceptions of political conduct and a wholly new environment, between the inadequacy of the nation-state and the emerging imperative of global community. In the past thirty years the world came to assume that a stable economic system and spreading prosperity would continue indefinitely. New nations launched themselves confidently on the path of economic and social development; technical innovation and industrial expansion promised steady improvement in the standard of living of all nations; surpluses of fuel, food and raw materials were considered a burden rather than a blessing. While poverty and misery still afflicted many parts of the globe, over the long run there was universal hope; the period was fairly characterized as a "revolution of rising expectations." That time has ended. Now there are fundamental questions about our capacity to meet even our most basic needs. In 1972, partly due to bad weather around the globe, world grain production declined for the first time in two decades. We were made ominously conscious of the thin edge between hope and hunger, and of the world's dependence on the surplus production of a few nations. In 1973 first a political embargo and then abruptly raised prices for oil curbed production in the world's factories and farms, and sharply accelerated a global inflation that was already at the margin of government's ability to control. In 1974, the international monetary and trading system continues under mounting stress, not yet able to absorb the accumulated weight of repeated shocks. Its institutions still struggling to respond. The same interdependence that brought common advance now threatens us with common decline.

We must act now and we must act together to regain control over our shared destiny. Catastrophe when it cannot be foreseen can be blamed on a failure of vision or on forces beyond our control. But the current trend is obvious and the remedy is within our power. If we do not act boldly, disaster will result from a failure of will; moral culpability will be inherent in our foreknowledge.

The political challenge is straightforward: Will the nations of the world cooperate to confront a crisis which is both self-evident and global in nature? Or will each nation or region or bloc see its special advantages as a weapon instead of as a contribution? Will we pool our strengths and progress together, or test our strengths and sink together?

President Ford has instructed me to declare on behalf of the United States: We regard our good fortune and strength in the field of food as a global trust. We recognize the responsibilities we bear by virtue of our extraordinary productivity, our advanced technology, and our tradition of assistance. That is why we proposed this conference. That is why a Secretary of State is giving this address. The United States will make a major effort to match its capacity to the magnitude of the challenge. We are convinced that the collective response will have an important influence on the nature of the world that our children inherit.

As we move toward the next century the nations assembled here must begin to fashion a global conception. For we are irreversibly linked to each other—by interdependent economies and human aspirations, by instant communications and nuclear peril. The contemporary agenda of energy, food and inflation exceeds the capacity of any single government, or even of a few governments together, to resolve.

All nations—east and west, north and south—are linked to a single economic system. Preoccupation with narrow advantage is foredoomed. It is bound to lead to sterile confrontations, undermining the international cooperation upon which achievement of national objectives depends. The poorest and weakest nations will suffer most. Discontent and instabilities will be magnified in all countries. New dangers will be posed to recent progress in reducing international tensions. But this need not be our future. There is great opportunity as well as grave danger in the present crisis. Recognition of our condition can disenthrall us from outdated conceptions, from institutional inertia, from sterile rivalries. If we comprehend our reality and act upon it, we can usher in a period of unprecedented advance with consequences far transcending the issues before this conference. We will have built an international system worthy of the capacities and aspiration of mankind.

We must begin here with the challenge of food. No social system, ideology or principle of justice can tolerate a world in which the spiritual and physical potential of hundreds of millions is stunted from elemental hunger or inadequate nutrition. National pride or regional suspicions lose any moral and practical justification if they prevent us from overcoming this scourge.

A generation ago many farmers were self-sufficient; today fuel, fertilizer, capital and technology are essential for their economic survival. A generation ago many nations were self-sufficient; today a good many exporters provide the margin between life and death for many millions.

Thus food has become a central element of the international economy. A world of energy shortages, rampant inflation, and a weakening trade and monetary system will be a world of food shortages as well. And food shortages in turn sabotage growth and accelerate inflation.

The food problem has two levels—first, coping with food emergency; and second, assuring long-term supplies and an adequate standard of nutrition for our growing populations.

During the 1950s and 60s global food production grew with great consistency. Per capita output expanded even in the food-deficit nations; the world's total output increased by more than half. But at the precise moment when growing populations and rising expectations made a continuation of this trend essential, a dramatic change occurred: During the past three years, world cereal production has fallen; reserves have dropped to the point where significant crop failure can spell a major disaster.

The longer-term picture is, if anything, starker still. Even today hundreds of millions of people do not eat enough for decent and productive lives. Since increases in production are not evenly distributed, the absolute number of malnourished people are, in fact, probably greater today than ever before except in times of famine. In many parts of the world 30 to 50 percent of the children die before the age of five, millions of them from malnutrition. Many survive only with permanent damage to their intellectual and physical capacities.

World population is projected to double by the end of the century. It is clear that we must meet the food need that this entails. But it is equally clear that population cannot continue indefinitely to double every generation. At some point we will inevitably exceed the earth's capacity to sustain human life. The near as well as the long-term challenges of food have three components:

There is the problem of production. In the face of population trends, maintaining even current inadequate levels of nutrition and food security will require that we produce twice as much food by the end of this century. Adequate nutrition would require 150 percent more food, or a total annual output of 3 billion tons of grain.

There is the problem of distribution. Secretary General Marei estimates that at the present rate of growth of 2.5 percent a year the gap between what the developing countries produce themselves and what they need will rise from 25 million to 85 million tons a year by 1985. For the foreseeable future, food will have to be transferred on a substantial scale from where it is in surplus to where it is in shortage.

There is the problem of reserves. Protection against the vagaries of weather and disaster urgently requires a food reserve. Our estimate is that as much as 60 million tons over current carry-over levels may be required.

In short, we are convinced that the world faces a challenge new in its severity, its pervasiveness, and its global dimension. Our minimum objective of the next quarter-century must be to more than double world food production and to improve its quality. To meet this objective the United States proposes to this conference a comprehensive program of urgent, cooperative worldwide action of five fronts:

increasing the production of food exporters
accelerating the production in developing countries
improving means of food distribution and financing
enhancing food quality
ensuring security against food emergencies

Let me deal with each of these in turn.

Increased Production by Food Exporters

A handful of countries, through good fortune and technology, can produce more than they need and thus are able to export. Reliance on this production is certain to grow through the next decade and perhaps beyond. Unless we are to doom the world to chronic famine, the major exporting nations must rapidly expand their potential and seek to ensure the dependable long-term growth of their supplies.

They must begin by adjusting their agricultural policies to a new economic reality. For years these policies were based on the premise that production to full capacity created undesirable surpluses and depressed markets, depriving farmers of incentives to invest and produce. It is now abundantly clear that this is not the problem we face; there is no surplus so long as there is an unmet need. In that sense, no real surplus has ever existed. The problem has always been a collective failure to transfer apparent surpluses to areas of shortages. In current and foreseeable conditions this can surely be accomplished without dampening incentives for production in either area.

The United States has taken sweeping steps to expand its output to the maximum. It already has 167 million acres under grain production alone, an increase of 23 million acres from two years ago. In an address to the Congress last month, President Ford asked for a greater effort still; he called upon every American farmer to produce to full capacity. He directed the elimination of all restrictive practices which raise food prices; he assured farmers that he will use present authority and seek additional authority to allocate the fuel and fertilizer they require; and he urged the removal of remaining acreage limitations.

These efforts should be matched by all exporting countries. Maximum production will require a substantial increase in investment. The best land, the most accessible water, and the most obvious improvements are already in use. Last year the United States raised its investment in agriculture by $2.5 billion. The United States government is launching a systematic survey of additional investment requirements and of ways to ensure that they are met.

A comparable effort by other nations is essential. The United States believes that cooperative action among exporting countries is required to stimulate rational planning and the necessary increases in output. We are prepared to join with other major exporters in a common commitment to raise production, to make the necessary investment, and to begin rebuilding reserves for food security. Immediately following the conclusion of this conference, the United States proposes to convene a group of major exporters—an export planning group—to shape a concrete and coordinated program to achieve these goals.

Accelerated Production of Developing Countries

The food exporting nations alone will simply not be able to meet the world's basic needs. Ironically but fortunately, it is the nations with the most rapidly growing food deficits which also possess the greatest capacity for increased production. They have the largest amounts of unused land and water. While they now have 35 percent more land in grain production than the developed nations, they produce 20 percent less on this land. In short, the largest growth in world food production can—and must—take place in the chronic deficit countries.

Yet the gap between supply and demand in these countries is growing, not narrowing. At the current growth rate, the grain supply deficit is estimated to more than triple and reach some 85 million tons by 1985. To cut this gap in half would require accelerating their growth rate from the historically high average of 2.5 percent per annum to 3.5 percent—an increase in the rate of growth of 40 percent.

Two key areas need major emphasis to achieve even this minimum goal: new research and new investment.

International and national research programs must be concentrated on the special needs of the chronic food-deficit nations and they must be intensified. New technologies must be developed to increase yields and reduce costs, making use of the special features of their labor-intensive, capital-short economies.

On the international plane, we must strengthen and expand the research network linking the less developed countries with research institutions in the industrialized

countries and with the existing eight international agricultural research centers. We propose that resources for these
centers be more than doubled by 1980. For its part the
United States will in the same period triple its own contribution for the international centers, for agricultural research efforts in the less developed countries, and for
research by American universities on the agricultural problems of developing nations. The existing Consultative
Group on International Agricultural Research can play an
important coordinating role in this effort.

The United States is gratified by the progress of two
initiatives which we proposed at the sixth special session of
the UN General Assembly last April: the international Fertilizer Development Center and the study on the impact of
climate change on food supply. The fertilizer center opened
its doors last month in the United States with funds provided by Canada and the United States: We invite wider
participation and pledge its resources to the needs of the
developing nations. And the important study on climate
and food supply has been taken on by the United Nations
World Meteorological Organization.

National as well as international research efforts must
be brought to bear. The United States offers to share with
developing nations the results of its advanced research. We
already have under way a considerable range of promising
projects: to increase the protein content of common cereals;
to fortify staple foods with inexpensive nutrients; to improve plant fixation of atmospheric nitrogen to reduce the
need for costly fertilizers; to develop new low-cost, small-
scale tools and machines for the world's millions of small
farmers.

We also plan a number of new projects. Next year, our
space, agriculture and weather agencies will test advanced
satellite techniques for surveying and forecasting important
food crops. We will begin in North America and then
broaden the project to other parts of the world. To supplement the WMO study on climate, we have begun our own

analysis of the relationship between climatic patterns and crop yields over a statistically significant period. This is a promising and potentially vital contribution to rational planning of global production.

The United States will also make available the results of these projects for other nations.

Finally, President Ford is requesting the National Academy of Sciences, in cooperation with the Department of Agriculture and other governmental agencies, to design a far-reaching food and nutrition research program to mobilize America's talent. It is the President's aim to dedicate America's resources and America's scientific talent to finding new solutions, commensurate both with the magnitude of the human need and the wealth of our scientific capacities.

While we can hope for technological breakthroughs, we cannot count on them. There is no substitute for additional investment in chronic food-deficit countries. New irrigation systems, storage and distribution systems, production facilities for fertilizer, pesticide and seed and agricultural credit institutions are all urgently needed. Much of this can be stimulated and financed locally. But substantial outside resources will be needed for some time to come.

The United States believes that investment should be concentrated in strategic areas, applying existing, and in some cases very simple, technologies to critical variables in the process of food production. Among these are fertilizer, better storage facilities and pesticides.

Modern fertilizer is probably the most critical single input for increasing crop yields; it is also the most dependent on new investment. In our view fertilizer production is an ideal area for collaboration between wealthier and poorer nations, especially combining the technology of the developed countries, the capital and raw materials of the oil producers and the growing needs of the least developed countries. Existing production capacity is inadequate worldwide; new fertilizer industries should be created especially in the developing countries to meet local and regional needs for the long term. This could be done most efficiently on the basis of regional cooperation.

The United States will strongly support such regional efforts. In our investment and assistance programs we will give priority to the building of fertilizer industries and will share our advanced technology.

Another major priority must be to reduce losses from inadequate storage, transport, and pest control. Tragically, as much as 15 percent of a country's food production is often lost after harvesting because of pests that attack grains in substandard storage facilities. Better methods of safe storage must be taught and spread as widely as possible. Existing pesticides must be made more generally available. Many of these techniques are simple and inexpensive; investment in these areas could have a rapid and substantial impact on the world's food supply.

To plan a coherent investment strategy, the United States proposes the immediate formation of a coordinating group for food production and investment. We recommend that the World Bank join with the Food and Agricultural Organization and the UN Development Program to convene such a group this year. It should bring together representatives from both traditional donors and new financial powers, from multilateral agencies and from developing countries, with the following mandate:

To encourage bilateral and international assistance programs to provide the required external resources

To help governments stimulate greater internal resources for agriculture

To promote the most effective uses of new investment by the chronic deficit countries

The United States has long been a major contributor to agricultural development. We intend to expand this contribution. We have reordered our development assistance priorities to place the central emphasis on food and nutri-

tion programs. We have requested an increase of almost
$350 million for them in our current budget. This new em-
phasis will continue for as long as the need exists.

For all these international measures to be effective, governments must reexamine their overall agricultural policies
and practices. Outside countries can assist with technology
and the transfer of resources; the setting of priorities properly remains the province of national authorities. In far too
many countries, farmers have no incentive to make the investment required for increased production because prices
are set at unremunerative levels, because credit is unavail-
able, or because transportation and distribution facilities
are inadequate. Just as the exporting countries must adjust
their own policies to new realities, so must developing countries give a higher priority for food production in their development budgets and in their tax, credit and investment
policies.

Improving Food Distribution and Financing

While we must urgently produce more food, the problem
of its distribution will remain crucial. Even with maximum
foreseeable agricultural growth in the developing countries,
their food import requirement is likely to amount to some
40 million tons a year in the mid-1980s, or nearly twice the
current level.

How is the cost of these imports to be met?

The earnings of the developing countries themselves, of
course, remain the principal source. The industrialized nations can make a significant contribution simply by improving access to their markets. With the imminent passage of
the trade bill, the United States reaffirms its commitment
to institute a system of generalized tariff preferences for the
developing nations and to pay special attention to their
needs in the coming multilateral trade negotiations.

Nevertheless, an expanded flow of food aid will clearly
be necessary. During this fiscal year, the United States will
increase its food-aid contribution, despite the adverse

weather conditions which have affected our crops. The American people have a deep and enduring commitment to help feed the starving and the hungry. We will do everything humanly possible to assure that our future contribution will be responsive to the growing needs.

The responsibility for financing food imports cannot, however, rest with the food exporters alone. Over the next few years in particular, the financing needs of the food-deficit developing countries will simply be too large for either their own limited resources or the traditional food-aid donors.

The oil exporters have a special responsibility in this regard. Many of them have income far in excess of that needed to balance their international payments or to finance their economic development. The continuing massive transfer of wealth and the resulting impetus to worldwide inflation have shattered the ability of the developing countries to purchase food, fertilizer and other goods. And the economic crisis has severely reduced the imports of the industrialized countries from the developing nations.

The United States recommends that the traditional donors and the new financial powers participating in the coordinating group for food production and investment make a major effort to provide the food and funds required. They could form a subcommittee on food financing which, as a first task, would negotiate a minimum global quantity of food for whose transfer to food-deficit developing countries over the next three years they are prepared to find the necessary finances.

I have outlined various measures to expand production, to improve the earning capacity of developing countries, to generate new sources of external assistance. But it is not clear that even these measures will be sufficient to meet the longer-term challenge, particularly if our current estimates of the gap by 1985 and beyond prove to be too conservative.

Therefore, ways must be found to move more of the surplus oil revenue into long-term lending or grants to the poorer countries. The United States proposes that the development committee, created at the recent session of the governors of the International Bank and Monetary Fund, be charged with the urgent study of whether existing sources of financing are sufficient to meet the expected import requirements of developing countries. If these sources are not sufficient, new means must be found to supplement them. This must become one of the priority objectives of the countries and institutions that have the major influence in the international monetary system.

Enhancing Food Quality

Supplies alone do not guarantee man's nutritional requirements. Even in developed countries, with ample supplies, serious health problems are caused by the wrong kinds and amounts of food. In developing countries, the problem is magnified. Not only inadequate distribution but also the rising cost of food dooms the poorest and most vulnerable groups—children and mothers—to inferior quality as well as insufficient quantity of food. Even with massive gains in food production, the world could still be haunted by the specter of inadequate nutrition.

First, we must understand the problem better. We know a good deal about the state of global production. But our knowledge of the state of global nutrition is abysmal. Therefore the United States proposes that a global nutrition surveillance system be established by the World Health Organization, the Food and Agricultural Organization and the United Nations International Children's Emergency Fund. Particular attention should be devoted to the special needs of mothers and young children and to responding quickly to local emergencies affecting these particularly vulnerable groups. Nutrition surveying is a field with which the United States has considerable experience; we are ready to share our knowledge and techniques.

Second, we need new methods for combating malnutrition. The United States invites the WHO, FAO and

UNICEF to arrange for an internationally coordinated program in applied nutritional research. Such a program should set priorities, identify the best centers for research, and generate the necessary funding. The United States is willing to contribute $5 million to initiate such a program.

Third, we need to act on problems which are already clear. The United States proposes an immediate campaign against two of the most prevalent and blighting effects of malnutrition: Vitamin A blindness and iron-deficiency anemia. The former is responsible for well over half of the millions of cases of blindness in less developed countries; the current food shortages will predictably increase this number. Iron-deficiency anemia is responsible for low productivity in many parts of the world.

Just as the world has come close to eradicating smallpox, yellow fever and polio, it can conquer these diseases. There are available new and relatively inexpensive techniques which could have a substantial impact. The United States is ready to cooperate with developing countries and international donors to carry out the necessary programs. We are prepared to contribute $10 million to an international effort.

Finally, we need to reflect our concern for food quality in existing programs. This conference should devote special attention to food aid programs explicitly designed to fight malnutrition among the most vulnerable groups. The United States will increase funding for such programs by at least $50 million this year.

Ensuring Against Food Emergencies

The events of the past few years have brought home the grave vulnerability of mankind to food emergencies caused by crop failures, floods, wars and other disasters. The world has come to depend on a few exporting countries, and particularly the United States, to maintain the necessary reserves. But reserves no longer exist, despite the fact that the United States has removed virtually all of its restrictions on production and our farmers have made an all-out effort to maximize output. A worldwide reserve of as much as 60 million tons of food above present carry-over levels may be needed to assure adequate food security.

It is neither prudent nor practical for one or even a few countries to be the world's sole holder of reserves. Nations with a history of radical fluctuations in import requirements have an obligation, both to their own people and to the world community, to participate in a system which shares that responsibility more widely. And exporting countries can no longer afford to be caught by surprise. They must have advance information to plan production and exports.

We commend FAO Director General Boerma for his initiative in the area of reserves. The United States shares his view that a cooperative multilateral system is essential for greater equity and efficiency. We therefore propose that this conference organize a reserves coordinating group to negotiate a detailed agreement on an international system of nationally held grain reserves at the earliest possible time. It should include all the major exporters as well as those whose import needs are likely to be greatest. This group's work should be carried out in close cooperation with other international efforts to improve the world trading system.

An international reserve system should include the following elements:

exchange of information on levels of reserve and working stocks, on crop prospects and on intentions regarding imports or exports;

agreement on the size of global reserves required to protect against famine and price fluctuations;

sharing of the responsibility for holding reserves;

guidelines on the management of national reserves, defining the conditions for adding to reserves and for releasing from them;

preference for cooperating countries in the distribution of reserves;

procedures for adjustment of targets and settlements of disputes and measures for dealing with noncompliance.

Agenda for the Future

The challenge before this conference is to translate needs into programs and programs into results. We have no time to lose.

I have set forth a five-point platform for joint action:

to concert the efforts of the major surplus countries to help meet the global demand;

to expand the capacity of chronic food-deficit developing nations for growth and greater self-sufficiency;

to transfer resources and food to meet the gaps which remain;

to improve the quality of food to ensure adequate nutrition;

to safeguard men and nations from sudden emergencies and the vagaries of weather.

I have outlined the contribution that the United States is prepared to make in national or multilateral programs to achieve each of these goals. And I have proposed three new international groups to strengthen national efforts, coordinate them and give them global focus:

the Exporters Planning Group;

the Food Production and Investment Coordinating Group;

the Reserves Coordinating Group.

A number of suggestions have been made for a central body to fuse our efforts and provide leadership. The United States is open-minded about such an institution. We strongly believe, however, that whatever the mechanisms, a unified, concerted and comprehensive approach is an absolute requirement. The American delegation headed by our distinguished Secretary of Agriculture Earl Butz is prepared to begin urgent discussions to implement our proposals. We welcome the suggestions of other nations gathered here. We will work hard and we will work cooperatively.

Nothing more overwhelms the human spirit, or mocks our values and our dreams, than the desperate struggle for sustenance. No tragedy is more wounding than the look of despair in the eyes of a starving child.

Once famine was considered part of the normal cycle of man's existence, a local or at worst a national tragedy. Now our consciousness is global. Our achievements, our expectations, and our moral convictions have made this issue into a universal political concern.

The profound promise of our era is that for the first time we may have the technical capacity to free mankind from the scourge of hunger. Therefore, today we must proclaim a bold objective—that within a decade no child will go to bed hungry, that no family will fear for its next day's bread, and that no human being's future and capacities will be stunted by malnutrition.

Our responsibility is clear.

Let the nations gathered here resolve to confront the challenge, not each other.

Let us agree that the scale and severity of the task require a collaborative effort unprecedented in history.

And let us make global cooperation in food a model for our response to other challenges of an interdependent world —energy, inflation, population, protection of the environment.

William Faulkner expressed the confidence that "man will not merely endure, he will prevail." We live today in a world so complex that even only to endure, man must prevail. Global community is no longer a sentimental ideal but a practical necessity. National purposes, international realities and human needs all summon man to a new test of his capacity and his morality.

We cannot turn back or turn away.

"Human reason," Thomas Mann wrote, "needs only to will more strongly than fate and it is fate."

FEAST OR FAMINE: THE KEY TO PEACE [3]

Earl L. Butz [4]

About four weeks after the Rome food conference, Earl L. Butz, Secretary of Agriculture, addressed 2,500 persons at a banquet of the fifty-sixth annual convention of the Iowa Farm Bureau Meeting, December 10, 1974, at the Veterans Auditorium in Des Moines. To promise aid in Rome was much easier than to justify the program in the agricultural Middle West. In the Ford Administration, Butz has the responsibility of keeping the farmers happy. Of course Butz was speaking in the home state of Senator Dick Clark, with whom he had had some disagreement in Rome. There Democratic members of the American delegation of forty—Senators Clark, George McGovern of South Dakota, and Hubert Humphrey of Minnesota—had embarrassed the Administration by urging it to increase its food allotment from one to two million tons for international distribution. At a press conference in Rome, Butz had charged that the Democrats were acting "for partisan political gains."

The Administration, of course, facing consumers enraged by high prices, was not eager to drive prices up by announcing the increase of shipments of food abroad. It was perhaps this squabble (see *Congressional Record,* November 19, 1974, p S 19549; November 25, 1974, p S 20147–S 20158; December 9, 1974, p S 20769–S 20774) that caused Butz to say early in his presentation, "The Rome conference was filled with rhetoric—much of it for home consumption." Consistent with his earlier speeches, Butz emphasized that the farmer could become "an effective hunger fighter" by engaging in full production. To cope with isolationist sentiments, strong in the farm belt, Butz stressed that the contribution of food to feed the hungry was a good way to avoid war.

Butz has been called "the farmer's friend and cantankerous defender of free enterprise in the agricultural marketplace" (Bill Granger, *Britannica Yearbook, 1974,* p 130). He is much in demand as a speaker at banquets and farm functions. According to *Current Biography* (July 1972), Butz ". . . has . . . a quick tongue and an energetic, genial disposition." He has a tenor voice, a crisp

[3] Delivered at the fifty-sixth annual convention of the Iowa Farm Bureau Meeting, Veterans Auditorium, Des Moines, Iowa, December 10, 1974. Quoted by permission.

[4] For biographical note, see Appendix.

enunciation, and speaks at a fairly rapid rate. According to Julius Duscha (New York *Times Magazine,* April 16, 1972, p 34), he is a "clever platform performer, who sprinkles his speeches with barnyard humor, hoary jokes, and country talk, all of which delights his rural audiences." There is little doubt that he is direct, forceful, articulate, courageous, and at times obstinate and dogmatic.

In the speech included here he shows his style when he says, "One can always leave the car in the garage if the gas tank is empty, but if there isn't a little rice in the bowl or bread on the plate, we can get into trouble pretty fast." Later on he says, "We feel that a farmer responds to financial incentives in about the same way whether he farms with a forked stick in India or rides a $20,000 tractor in Iowa." His Iowa audience enjoyed his homespun language and interrupted him several times with applause. Those attending that banquet appeared to be in general agreement with what the secretary proposed. It may seem ironic that starvation was the subject of a banquet speech.

Like Secretary of State Henry Kissinger, Butz undoubtedly has able speech assistants that assemble his materials and cast many of his paragraphs. But, his speeches reflect his personality and rhetorical characteristics.

Some four weeks ago, about two thousand delegates from approximately 130 nations assembled in Rome for the World Food Conference. As never before experienced in this type of international convocation, attention was focused on food as the key to affluence, to health, to happiness, and, indeed, to world peace.

Food-surplus nations sat beside food-deficit nations; wealthy nations beside poor nations; developed nations beside developing nations; well-fed nations beside nations living intimately with human starvation; and the highly nourished nations next to the malnourished. All had the same common objective of raising the levels of nutrition for all people, to find a more equitable system of global food distribution, and to set up a mechanism that will prevent a recurrence of the critical food situation in which many parts of the world find themselves today.

While one cannot completely assess such an undertaking so soon after it happened, I am confident that ten years hence we will look back on the Rome food conference and view it as a milestone in man's long battle against hunger and human misery.

Like many international conferences, the Rome conference was filled with rhetoric—much of it for home consumption. Unlike many international conferences, however, the Rome meeting provided for postconference committees and mechanisms to implement the recommendations growing out of the conference itself. The United States will be a full and active participant in these sessions and will continue to make constructive and valuable contributions.

The Rome conference zeroed in on half a dozen important areas. Briefly, they were:

Food Production. There was agreement that increased food production is essential in both developed and developing areas. Additional funds to stimulate production in developing countries will be required and means were discussed for establishing such funds.

Food Aid. The conference recommended that food-aid donor countries make all efforts, beginning in 1975, to provide commodities and/or financial assistance to ensure at least 10 million tons of grain per year as food aid.

World Food Security. The conference endorsed the Food and Agriculture Organization's undertaking for international cooperation in establishing a world network of national grain reserves.

Information. It was decided to establish a Global Information and Early Warning System on Food and Agriculture—essential to the whole objective of improved food security around the world.

Trade. The conference stressed the need for eliminating trade barriers.

World Food Council. It approved establishment through the United Nations of a World Food Council to have coordinating, consultative and advisory powers with respect to food aid, investment and other foreign assistance.

I was pleased with this progress, but it also left a great deal of work to be done.

The Rome conference and other events over the past year or so have proved that the two most critical problems in the world today are food and fuel shortages. But perhaps food is the most important of the two. One can always leave the car in the garage if the gas tank is empty, but if there isn't a little rice in the bowl or bread on the plate, we can get into trouble pretty fast.

Consequently, if there was any single dominant theme coming out of the Rome meetings, it dealt with the need for increased production all over the world. Many participants pointed out that the opportunities for increased production are perhaps greater in the developing countries than in the developed.

The need in these developing countries is for massive inputs of technical assistance, of research, of technology, and of capital. They need to give food production a much higher position on their priority scale than has often been the case in the past. It may have been nice for government officials to point to a new steel mill or a jumbo jet in their national airline's fleet, but these symbols of industrial advancement didn't help much in a country where perhaps three fourths of the people live on the land while hunger yet walks side by side with half of the population.

When food is such a central problem, we all ought to be grateful that the United States is far and away the world's leading food producing nation and the world's leading food export nation. Our food policy should be a model to the world. It is one of full production, with no cartel pricing and with equal access to our supplies by users both here at home and abroad.

We pointed out to our fellow delegates that one of the reasons food production is so high in the United States is that our system provides an incentive for farmers to invest, to innovate, to expand, and to take commercial risks. We tried to emphasize that it is little wonder in some nations that increases in food production come haltingly when those nations follow an internal cheap food policy that holds prices down to producers. We feel that a farmer responds to financial incentives in about the same way whether he farms with a forked stick in India or rides a $20,000 tractor in Iowa.

Only farmers produce food. World food conferences don't produce food; governments don't produce food; state farm bureaus don't produce food; politicians don't produce food. Only a farmer and his family on the land produce food. The essential challenge, therefore, is to provide that farmer and his family with the incentive that will make him strive to excel and to give him the infrastructure that will permit him to maximize production from the land and labor available to him.

We have succeeded remarkably well in the United States in doing this. No civilization or society has ever matched what American agriculture has done in the twentieth century. The increase in productivity of the American farmer since the close of the last world war is nothing short of phenomenal.

Comparing the years 1950–54 with the years 1970–74, we can get some idea of what has been accomplished. In that short span total farm output has increased by 42 percent. The increase in output has gone up with productivity, and productivity in the 1970–74 period increased 43 percent over the levels of 1950–54. Clearly, agriculture has been one of the most rapidly productive sectors of the American economy.

These advances have been the primary reasons why the American farmer can now feed 213 million Americans better than ever before in our history. Farmers can now feed twice as many Americans as they did 50 years ago on 6 percent fewer acres than were harvested 50 years ago. What

makes that even more meaningful is that we are today feed-
ing hundreds of millions of people around the world as
well as ourselves—something we were not doing to the same
degree half a century ago.

I believe there is a simple explanation for this record.
The American farmer has been encouraged to invest in his
operation and to innovate. He has been encouraged to apply the latest technological and scientific developments. In
short, to take a little risk in the hope of increasing his returns.

The basic farm policy of the United States has been completely turned around in the last couple of years. As we
now go for full production with market price orientation,
we are in sharp contrast with the last three or four decades.
Briefly, let me summarize this change as I perceive it.

It has moved:

(1) from high internal price supports to a system of market price orientation;

(2) from curtailed production to full output;

(3) from production allotments and quotas to freedom
from producer allotments;

(4) from heavy dependence on government to primary
dependence on the marketplace;

(5) from broad governmental controls to minimal or no
controls;

(6) from heavy government stocks to vanishing govern-
ment-held stocks;

(7) from a moderate level of agricultural exports in world
trade to a major contribution of agricultural exports to
world trade.

In sum, our policy now is full utilization of the marvel-
ous God-given agricultural resources in our country and
will result in some very basic accomplishments. It will:

assure the American population an adequate food supply at the most reasonable possible prices;

continue to provide America's most important single source of foreign exchange;

permit America, through the export route, to raise the levels of nutrition of hundreds of millions of people around the world through commercial channels of trades;

permit America to continue her historic role of being a good neighbor in the world community of nations.

There are a number of nations in a truly critical food situation. If relief doesn't come, governments could topple. Food riots might occur. Local unrest may grow into full-blown revolutions. And revolutions, once started, are difficult to contain. No longer can any nation of the world, and especially any affluent nation, enjoy the political isolation from the rest of the world that may have been possible a half a century ago.

This situation places the United States, sooner or later, in the middle of any world disturbance. In recognition of this, in the last decade especially, the United States has truly become the world's peace broker. This is a relatively new role for our country. Sometimes we play it awkwardly, though nonetheless sincerely. We covet no new territory. We seek to conquer no people. We don't seek to impose our religion, or our social customs, or even our form of government on other peoples. We seek only peace and tranquillity.

On at least four occasions in this century, we have been engulfed in deadly struggle beyond our borders. On each occasion the food that our farmers produced played a central role in total American strength and in ultimate victory.

The challenge now is not to use American food for victory in war. The challenge is to use American food and expertise for victory in peace. The challenge is to mobilize all the nations of the world in an effort to conquer mankind's age-old quest for better eating, for better health, for better living.

It is on this very front that the American farmer can truly become an effective hunger fighter. It is on this very front that the American farmer can help his counterpart, whether he be a brown-skinned Indian, a yellow-skinned Thai, or a dark-skinned Kenyan. It is on this very front that the American farmer can wage war against the malnutrition that causes youngsters to have inflated abdomens; against conditions which prevent mothers from producing even enough milk for minimal growth of shriveled infants; against situations which condemn individuals to go through life as mental invalids because of nutritional deficiencies in their childhood years.

Mahatma Gandhi, the Indian philosopher of more than a generation ago, very wisely remarked one day: "Even God dare not approach a hungry man except in the form of bread." One need not travel far these days to understand why bread is the most powerful of all languages. It is a universal language. It is a language that growing millions yearn to hear and a language that nations will heed. It is precisely the language that the United States is prepared to speak, powerfully and eloquently. It is a language we are still learning to speak, sometimes awkwardly. It is the language we must speak louder and louder, year by year. It is the language of peace.

GLOBAL INTERDEPENDENCE: "LIFE, LIBERTY, AND THE PURSUIT OF HAPPINESS" IN TODAY'S WORLD [5]

Mark O. Hatfield [6]

Senator Mark O. Hatfield (Republican, Oregon) argues that "protecting and preserving the life of citizens in America is directly dependent upon the conditions that will preserve and nurture life throughout the world. . . . We are tied together with mankind in a single destiny."

This statement suggests the growing awareness that no one nation can solve its problems or save the starving millions scattered across the globe. In a speech included in REPRESENTATIVE AMERICAN SPEECHES: 1973–1974, anthropologist Margaret Mead said the same thing: "There is only a common need to reassess our present course, to change that course and to devise new methods through which the whole world can survive."

On September 11, 1974, Senator Hatfield made a cogent speech on the need for international cooperation before the annual dinner of the Members of the Congress for Peace Through Law, in the Dirksen Senate Office Building, Washington, D.C. He spoke to an audience of about 150 persons, including fellow legislators (about 12 Senators and 50 Representatives).

Developing the speech around the phrase "life, liberty, and the pursuit of happiness" from the Declaration of Independence provided unity and enabled the speaker to associate his presentation on international affairs with the two hundredth anniversary of the Declaration of Independence. As usual, Senator Hatfield chose a rhetoric that was clear, and at the same time exciting and moving. The Oregon Senator is among the best of our senatorial and political speakers today. (For other speeches by Senator Hatfield, see REPRESENTATIVE AMERICAN SPEECHES: 1972–1973, p 91–3; and 1973–1974, p 105–8.)

Constantly we hear the term *national security* invoked to justify policies and programs as if no other explanation

---

[5] Delivered at the annual dinner of the Members of the Congress for Peace Through Law, Dirksen Senate Office Building, Washington, D.C., September 11, 1974. Quoted by permission.

[6] For biographical note, see Appendix.

is necessary. What we must do is define exactly what we mean by this term. It is a prevalent and frequent mistake to assume that our nation's security is wholly identical to our military might. That can be a component, but only one component, of what constitutes, in reality, our "national security."

Fundamentally, the security of our nation means the guarantee that we can live in a way and under a government that is committed to insure us the rights, as endowed by our Creator, of "life, liberty, and the pursuit of happiness." The threats to those basic rights can come from numerous sources both within and without the nation. Social disintegration, ecological deterioration, economic erosion, morally destitute corporate values held as a people, domestic and international injustice, and worldwide forces of instability are a few of the threats to our nation's security apart from the military power of governments whose ideology is hostile to our own.

Further, it is these other threats which, in fact, seem far more imminent to the fundamental rights and qualities that define our security. Thus, we should analyze with care precisely what it means to preserve and insure the ideals of "life, liberty, and the pursuit of happiness" in today's world.

There is one central truth we must realize: Protecting and preserving the life of citizens in America is directly dependent upon the conditions that will preserve and nurture life throughout the world. This increases as we realize the finite limitations to the resources necessary to preserve life. In an ultimate but very real way, the conditions for securing life here in America are dependent upon conditions and resources for sustaining life everywhere. We are tied together with mankind in a single destiny.

A major threat, economically and even militarily, to our national well-being and the world's peace is posed by the division between those, like us, with a monopoly of the world's basic resources, and those struggling to allow their people to eat and live. Such a world is inherently prone to violence, and provides no guarantee to security for either the rich or the poor. The greatest threat to wars in the future will stem from potential "wars of redistribution" for the world's wealth and resources.

Consider our past quest for security. Since World War II all the nations of the world have spent $3,699 trillion in this quest. The United States alone has spent half of that amount, or about the same as all the other nations of the world combined. With our nuclear arsenals, man possesses the capability of releasing explosive power equivalent to fifteen tons of TNT for every man, woman, and child on the face of the earth. In a world of nearly 4 billion people, there exists the capacity of destroying 400 billion people. In a matter of a moment, a thermonuclear explosion 3,000 times as large as the bomb dropped on Hiroshima can be directed to any point on the globe.

America is the number one military power in the world. Yet, we are fourteenth in the infant mortality. We are eighth in the ratio of doctors per patients. We are twenty-second in life expectancy. We are fourteenth in literacy.

The US budgets for military spending have continued to rise, over and above inflation, despite the end of the war. Further, this is the first time in recent history that military spending has risen following a war; after World War II and following the Korean war, there was a marked decline in our defense budgets. But today, we are spending more in "peace" than we were in "war."

Winston Churchill once said that increasing nuclear strength serves only to "make rubble bounce." Yet we have continued to increase our nuclear forces in what we call a quest for "security." Further, we still believe that security is primarily a function of military strength and international diplomacy. However, it is becoming more and more clear that the forces shaping our nation's and the world's real security go far beyond what can be even insured by treaties and arms.

We must accept the growing global interdependence of

the world, and also recognize the position of dominance and frequent exploitation that has characterized our role. So far, total US investment in developing nations has been very profitable, far more so than US investment in industrialized nations. The United States invested $16.23 billion in Europe and $10.9 billion in Canada from 1959 to 1969. Repatriated profits for these investments amounted to $7.3 billion from Europe and $4.7 billion from Canada for the ten-year period. However, in the third world nations of Latin America, Africa, and the Middle East, US investment from 1959 to 1969 amounted to $5.8 billion. Repatriated profits from these investments were $15.1 billion, more than a 250 percent return. This situation may very well change, however, as the poor countries of the world realize how dependent the industrialized nations are upon the third world's natural resources, and begin to charge prices more in keeping with the demand.

Consider the United States' dependence on the mineral resources of the poor countries. Like other rich countries that industrialized early, the United States has sorely depleted its indigenous sources of basic industrial raw materials. Thus we have reached an era of growing dependence on the largely unexploited mineral reserves of the poor countries. Of the thirteen basic industrial raw materials we require, the United States in 1950 was dependent on imports for more than half of its supplies of four—these were aluminum, manganese, nickel, and tin. By 1970, zinc and chromium were added, bringing to six the number of raw materials for which we were dependent on imports for more than half of our supplies. By 1985, the list will grow to nine as iron, lead, and tungsten are added. By the year 2000, we will depend on foreign sources for more than half of our supply of each of the thirteen raw materials except phosphate. Most of these sources are third world developing nations, such as Bolivia, Peru, Chile, Zambia, Zaïre, Ghana, and Nigeria.

Will the developing nations of the world continue to

abide the demands put on them to fuel the industrialized nations when they have their own very real needs at home? I believe not, especially when the demands of the industrialized nations arise out of wasteful consumer consumption and ever-increasing military budgets.

Although Americans comprise only 6 percent of the world's population, we consume 40 percent of the world's resources, and one third of the world's total energy. Our society is awash in more and more consumer goods designed for the affluent society, and sold to us by advertising techniques that even try to induce these "needs" within the public. Our consumptive style of abundance and waste contributes to the inequity and exploitation of the poor.

What pierces any sensitive heart most deeply is the suffering of the hungry of the world. Most of humanity is hungry. This is a daily struggle for millions of people, at home and throughout the world. Each day literally thousands lose that struggle and die of starvation. One third to one half of the world's people suffer from continual hunger or nutritional deprivation, and its effects. During a year, our diets require a ton of grain to support our consumption of meat, poultry, dairy products, and other ways of getting protein. But the person in a poorer country has only four hundred pounds of grain available each year for his diet. It takes five times the limited resources of land, water, and fertilizer to support our diet than to support the diet of a Nigerian, or Colombian, or Indian, or Chinese.

It is crucial we realize that there are limits to the "size of the pie." Famine will not be averted by simply thinking we can just increase the pie. Most arable land in the world is in use. The seas are being "overfished." The pie is limited, and it must be shared more equitably.

So what does all this mean? We can no longer suppose that our extra abundance—the crumbs from our table—can feed the hungry of the world. Rather, the world will be fed only by the sharing of resources which the rich of the world have assumed to be their unquestioned possession, and through the changing of values and patterns of life which the affluent have barely questioned.

At least 60 percent of all those 2.5 billion people living in the poorer, developing world are malnourished. We have not even touched on how malnutrition leads to death through disease for millions of people. One can have enough food to keep himself alive, but malnourished, making him far more susceptible to disease and death. Even more tragic is the evidence that malnutrition during a mother's pregnancy and the first months of an infant's life can cause permanent damage to the mental abilities of the child.

The world produces enough food to feed all its inhabitants. But when one third of the world's population—all those who are comparatively the "rich"—consume two thirds of the world's protein resources, then millions of the other two thirds of the world suffer, starve, and die.

Gandhi put it cogently and well: "The earth provides enough for everyman's need, but not for everyman's greed." There is no problem faced by this world more likely to breed instability and conflict, threatening our security and that of the entire world in the years ahead, than the disparity in distribution of food and basic resources for sustaining life.

To add to this global picture, we see that the gaps between the rich and the poor in the world have continued to widen. The gap between the per capita gross national products of the rich and poor nations was $2,000 in 1960. But currently, according to reports it approaches $3,000. Further, in the next thirty-five years the world's population is projected to double, with the greatest increases coming amongst the world's poor. Yet, in 1970, the world's military expenditures totaled $204 billion, a sum exceeding the entire income of the poorest half of mankind.

True peace is not the absence of conflict. It is the fulfillment of human needs. "Shalom" is the historic term embodying this vision of wholeness, fulfillment, and true peace. Our world will never know the hope for peace, and we will never have a generation of peace, until man can believe that the basic needs of life can be provided for him and for his children.

This is the vision of Members of Congress for Peace Through Law. We are trying to look at our world, not from the narrow perspective of blind nationalism, nor from the limited view of what the present seems to require, but rather from what is mandatory for mankind to survive in peace during the decades ahead of us. We believe that recognizing our interdependence and striving for a global community through law is the only alternative we have that leads to true security and peace. This is the overriding aim of all our efforts. These issues which will shape our future will be considered, in one way or another, by the Congress. Whether we act on them parochially, or from a global perspective, depends on how well our vision can be articulated to our colleagues in the Senate and House.

Recently, I read a frightening article. It suggested that the vision of the world today is like that of a lifeboat amidst a sea of people struggling to stay afloat. The lifeboat could only hold so many people, so those who were in had the right to keep the others out—to even beat them back with oars—in order for the boat to survive. The conclusion was that the rich of the world had the right not to make any room for the poor. Such a callous, inhumane view will be heard among those who cannot bear to face the realities of the future.

In contrast is the recognition of our common humanity: That we all inevitably ride together on spaceship earth; and that our destiny is linked together with all of God's children who inhabit the earth. This is the image which compassion instills in our hearts, and which can save our future.

We are approaching the two hundredth anniversary of the Declaration of Independence. Those men who signed that document saw the truth of their times, and were captured by a vision to which they pledged their lives, their

fortunes, and their sacred honor. Today, if we are to act in
that same spirit, we should issue a Declaration of Interdependence, pledging to it our lives, our fortunes, and our
sacred honor.

THE PRESS:
RIGHTS AND RESPONSIBILITIES

OR OF THE PRESS [1]

POTTER STEWART [2]

The press has never enjoyed greater power or prominence than at the present time. The investigative reporting of the war in Vietnam, the Watergate affair, and the Nixon Administration has demonstrated its effectiveness and importance. There is nevertheless evidence of growing antagonism and hostility toward reporters and a distrust of how the press uses its freedom.

This tension is discussed in a feature article in *Fortune* magazine (April 1975) entitled "The New Concerns About the Press." In part it points to the following problem:

> The deliberate politicization of news has become an endemic problem, especially among young reporters. There were occasions, especially in the late 1960s, when young reporters were so outraged by the Vietnam war, or the state of race relations in the United States, or the behavior of the police in Chicago, that they assumed a right to editorialize strenuously in their news stories. . . .
>
> The process implies some problems for the credibility of the press. Opinion polls reveal a more or less steady decline in public respect and trust accorded the news media (as well as all other institutions) since the early 1960s. Since there isn't any evidence that the press is less (or more) factually accurate than it used to be, the source of this credibility problem may be the newly controversial agenda and perspective being supplied by the national press.

Aware of this growing mood, Potter Stewart, Associate Justice of the United States Supreme Court, took as his subject "Or of the Press," at the sesquicentennial convocation at the Yale University Law School, November 2, 1974. It was a pleasant homecoming for the Justice because he had completed B.A. and LL.B. degrees, cum laude, at Yale and had served as editor of the *Yale*

---

[1] Delivered at the sesquicentennial convocation of the Yale University Law School, New Haven, Connecticut, November 2, 1974. Quoted by permission.

[2] For biographical note, see Appendix.

Law Journal. The formal occasion and an audience composed of
the law faculty and students, university officials, and other members of the staff and community demanded a formal address.

The Justice clearly set forth his thesis as follows:

> It is my thesis this morning that . . . the established Amer-
> ican press in the past ten years, and particularly in the past
> two years, has performed precisely the function it was in-
> tended to perform by those who wrote the First Amend-
> ment of our Constitution. I further submit that this thesis
> is supported by the relevant decisions of the Supreme
> Court.

The speech has a serious purpose of interpreting the law. In
a legalistic frame of reference the speaker traces the history of
freedom of press and cites relevant decisions pertaining to his
proposition. The speech is tight in its structure, well documented,
and logical in its development. He reaches his central point when
he affirms:

> The press is free to do battle against secrecy and deception
> in government. But the press cannot expect from the Con-
> stitution any guarantee that it will succeed. There is no
> constitutional right to have access to particular government
> information, or to require openness from the bureaucracy.
> The public's interest in knowing about its government is
> protected by the guarantee of a free press, but the protec-
> tion is indirect. The Constitution itself is neither a Freedom
> of Information Act nor an Official Secrets Act.
>
> The Constitution, in other words, establishes the contest,
> not its resolution. Congress may provide a resolution, at
> least in some instances, through carefully drawn legislation.
> For the rest, we must rely, as so often in our system we
> must, on the tug and pull of the political forces in Ameri-
> can society.

Justice Stewart has offered an interpretation that will be
studied by lawyers, judges, and scholars interested in the First
Amendment. Although he emphasized that his conclusions were
his own and not those of the Supreme Court of the United
States, he is a member of the Court and what he says takes on
special significance. Contrary to his conservatism in criminal cases
and his advocacy of judicial restraint, Justice Stewart often votes
with the liberal wing of the Court in cases involving the First
Amendment and civil rights.

Mr. Justice White, President Brewster, Dean Goldstein,
Mr. Ruebhausen, ladies and gentlemen:

It is a pleasure to be here today with my colleague Byron White, and I am very grateful to him for his generous words of introduction. And it is, of course, a pleasure to participate with him and with all of you in this convocation marking the commencement of the sesquicentennial year of the Yale Law School.

Just how it is that this *is* the law school's 150th anniversary is a subject that I am happy to leave for others to explain. All I know is that it is supposed to have something to do with a couple of young men who, in the year 1824, persuaded a friendly printer to give their proprietary law school a little free advertising space in the Yale College catalog.

But many great institutions have had humble beginnings. Even the Roman Empire, you will remember, traced its history back to no more than two hungry little boys and a friendly wolf.

Yet, however obscure the origins of this law school may have been, all of us know that by the early years of this century it was emerging as an important center for legal study. And by the time my classmates and I showed up here as first-year students in 1938, the Yale Law School had long since been universally recognized as one of a very few great national law schools in the Western world.

Just to speak the names of those, now gone, in whose classrooms I sat during my three years as a student here is to call the roll of some of the most notable legal scholars and law teachers in our country's history: Charles Clark, Arthur Corbin, Edwin Borchard, George Dession, Ashbel Gulliver, Walton Hamilton, Underhill Moore, Harry Shulman, Roscoe Steffens, Wesley Sturges.

And, although we hardly realized it then, the law school's student body during those three years was quite a remarkable collection of people as well. The membership of a single student eating club during that three-year period included, as it turned out, the two members of the Supreme Court who are here today, a United States Sena-

tor, three members of the House of Representatives, two
governors of Pennsylvania, two secretaries of the army,
an undersecretary of defense, a nominee for the vice presidency of the United States, a Vice President of the United
States, and the incumbent President of the United States.

The Yale Law School of that era had already acquired
a distinctive reputation for its leadership in the so-called
realist movement. Yet it was a place then, as it is a place
now, where, in the words of Dean Goldstein, "widely
divergent theories of law and society were taught and de-
bated, a school which cannot be described as representing
an orthodoxy of left, center, or right." It was then, as it
is now, an exciting place and a challenging place, where
a teacher's reach sometimes exceeded a student's grasp and
where, as a result, every student was invited to stretch himself, in intellect and understanding, to heights and breadths
well beyond his previous experience. There was a tradition here then, as there is now, of free inquiry, of independent thought, and of skeptical examination of the very
foundations of existing law.

It is in that tradition that I turn this morning to an
inquiry into an aspect of constitutional law that has only
recently begun to engage the attention of the Supreme
Court. Specifically, I shall discuss the role of the organized
press—of the daily newspapers and other established news
media—in the system of government created by our Constitution.

It was less than a decade ago—during the Vietnam years
—that the people of our country began to become aware
of the twin phenomena on a national scale of so-called
investigative reporting and an adversary press—that is, a
press adversary to the executive branch of the federal government. And only in the two short years that culminated
last summer in the resignation of a President did we fully
realize the enormous power that an investigative and adversary press can exert.

The public opinion polls that I have seen indicate that

some Americans firmly believe that the former Vice President and former President of the United States were hounded out of office by an arrogant and irresponsible press that had outrageously usurped dictatorial power. And it seems clear that many more Americans, while appreciating and even applauding the service performed by the press in exposing official wrongdoing at the highest levels of our national government, are nonetheless deeply disturbed by what they consider to be the illegitimate power of the organized press in the political structure of our society. It is my thesis this morning that, on the contrary, the established American press in the past ten years, and particularly in the past two years, has performed precisely the function it was intended to perform by those who wrote the First Amendment of our Constitution. I further submit that this thesis is supported by the relevant decisions of the Supreme Court.

Surprisingly, despite the importance of newspapers in the political and social life of our country, the Supreme Court has not until very recently been called upon to delineate their constitutional role in our structure of government.

Our history is filled with struggles over the rights and prerogatives of the press, but these disputes rarely found their way to the Supreme Court. The early years of the Republic witnessed controversy over the constitutional validity of the short-lived Alien and Sedition Act, but the controversy never reached the Court. In the next half-century there was nationwide turmoil over the right of the organized press to advocate the then subversive view that slavery should be abolished. In Illinois a publisher was killed for publishing abolitionist views. But none of this history made First Amendment law because the Court had earlier held that the Bill of Rights applied only against the federal government, not against the individual states.

With the passage of the Fourteenth Amendment, the constitutional framework was modified, and by the 1920s

the Court had established that the protections of the First
Amendment extend against all government—federal, state,
and local.

The next fifty years witnessed a great outpouring of
First Amendment litigation, all of which inspired books
and articles beyond number. But, with few exceptions,
neither these First Amendment cases nor their commentators squarely considered the Constitution's guarantee of a
free press. Instead, the focus was on its guarantee of free
speech. The Court's decisions dealt with the rights of iso-
lated individuals, or of unpopular minority groups, to
stand up against governmental power representing an an-
gry or frightened majority. The cases that came to the
Court during those years involved the rights of the soapbox
orator, the nonconformist pamphleteer, the religious evan-
gelist. The Court was seldom asked to define the rights and
privileges, or the responsibilities, of the organized press.

In very recent years cases involving the established press
finally have begun to reach the Supreme Court, and they
have presented a variety of problems, sometimes arising in
complicated factual settings.

In a series of cases, the Court has been called upon to
consider the limits imposed by the free press guarantee
upon a state's common or statutory law of libel. As a result of those cases, a public figure cannot successfully sue
a publisher for libel unless he can show that the publisher
maliciously printed a damaging untruth.

The Court has also been called upon to decide whether
a newspaper reporter has a First Amendment privilege to
refuse to disclose his confidential sources to a grand jury.
By a divided vote, the Court found no such privilege to
exist in the circumstances of the cases before it.

In another noteworthy case, the Court was asked by the
Justice Department to restrain publication by the New
York *Times* and other newspapers of the so-called Penta-
gon Papers. The Court declined to do so.

In yet another case, the question to be decided was

whether political groups have a First Amendment or statutory right of access to the federally regulated broadcast channels of radio and television. The Court held there was no such right of access.

Last term the Court confronted a Florida statute that required newspapers to grant a "right of reply" to political candidates they had criticized. The Court unanimously held this statute to be inconsistent with the guarantees of a free press.

It seems to me that the Court's approach to all these cases has uniformly reflected its understanding that the free press guarantee is, in essence, a *structural* provision of the Constitution. Most of the other provisions in the Bill of Rights protect specific liberties or specific rights of individuals: freedom of speech, freedom of worship, the right to counsel, the privilege against compulsory self-incrimination, to name a few. In contrast, the free press clause extends protection to an institution. The publishing business is, in short, the only organized private business that is given explicit constitutional protection.

This basic understanding is essential, I think, to avoid an elementary error of constitutional law. It is tempting to suggest that freedom of the press means only that newspaper publishers are guaranteed freedom of expression. They *are* guaranteed that freedom, to be sure, but so are we all, because of the free speech clause. If the free press guarantee meant no more than freedom of expression, it would be a constitutional redundancy. Between 1776 and the drafting of our Constitution, many of the state constitutions contained clauses protecting freedom of the press while at the same time recognizing no general freedom of speech. By including both guarantees in the First Amendment, the founders quite clearly recognized the distinction between the two.

It is also a mistake to suppose that the only purpose of the constitutional guarantee of a free press is to insure that a newspaper will serve as a neutral forum for debate, a "marketplace for ideas," a kind of Hyde Park corner for the community. A related theory sees the press as a neutral conduit of information between the people and their elected leaders. These theories, in my view, again give insufficient weight to the institutional autonomy of the press that it was the purpose of the Constitution to guarantee.

In setting up the three branches of the federal government, the founders deliberately created an internally competitive system. As Mr. Justice Brandeis once wrote:

The [founders'] purpose was, not to avoid friction, but, by means of the inevitable friction incident to the distribution of the governmental powers among three departments, to save the people from autocracy.

The primary purpose of the constitutional guarantee of a free press was a similar one: to create a fourth institution outside the government as an additional check on the three official branches. Consider the opening words of the free press clause of the Massachusetts Constitution, drafted by John Adams: "The liberty of the press is essential to the security of the state."

The relevant metaphor, I think, is the metaphor of the fourth estate. What Thomas Carlyle wrote about the British government a century ago has a curiously contemporary ring:

Burke said there were three estates in Parliament; but, in the reporters' gallery yonder, there sat a fourth estate more important far than they all. It is not a figure of speech or witty saying; it is a literal fact—very momentous to us in these times.

For centuries before our revolution, the press in England had been licensed, censored, and bedeviled by prosecutions for seditious libel. The British Crown knew that a free press was not just a neutral vehicle for the balanced discussion of diverse ideas. Instead, the free press meant organized, expert scrutiny of government. The press was a conspiracy of the intellect, with the courage of numbers. This formidable check on official power was what the

British Crown had feared—and what the American founders decided to risk.

It is this constitutional understanding, I think, that provides the unifying principle underlying the Supreme Court's recent decisions dealing with the organized press.

Consider first the libel cases. Officials within the three governmental branches are, for all practical purposes, immune from libel and slander suits for statements that they make in the line of duty. This immunity, which has both constitutional and common law origins, aims to insure bold and vigorous prosecution of the public's business. The same basic reasoning applies to the press. By contrast, the Court has never suggested that the constitutional right of free *speech* gives an *individual* any immunity from liability for either libel or slander.

In the cases involving the newspaper reporters' claims that they had a constitutional privilege not to disclose their confidential news sources to a grand jury, the Court rejected the claims by a vote of five to four, or, considering Mr. Justice Powell's concurring opinion, perhaps by a vote of four and a half to four and a half. But if freedom of the press means simply freedom of speech for reporters, this question of a reporter's asserted right to withhold information would have answered itself. None of us —as individuals—has a "free speech" right to refuse to tell a grand jury the identity of someone who has given us information relevant to the grand jury's legitimate inquiry. Only if a reporter is a representative of a protected *institution* does the question become a different one. The members of the Court disagreed in answering the question, but the question did not answer itself.

The cases involving the so-called right of access to the press raised the issue whether the First Amendment allows government, or indeed *requires* government, to regulate the press so as to make it a genuinely fair and open "marketplace for ideas." The Court's answer was no to both questions. If a newspaper wants to serve as a neutral mar-

ketplace for debate, that is an objective which it is free
to choose. And, within limits, that choice is probably necessary to commercially successful journalism. But it is a
choice that government cannot constitutionally impose.

Finally the Pentagon Papers case involved the line between secrecy and openness in the affairs of government.
The question, or at least one question, was whether that
line is drawn by the Constitution itself. The Justice Department asked the Court to find in the Constitution a
basis for prohibiting the publication of allegedly stolen
government documents. The Court could find no such pro-
hibition. So far as the Constitution goes, the autonomous
press may publish what it knows, and may seek to learn
what it can.

But this autonomy cuts both ways. The press is free
to do battle against secrecy and deception in government.
But the press cannot expect from the Constitution any
guarantee that it will succeed. There is no constitutional
right to have access to particular government information,
or to require openness from the bureaucracy. The public's
interest in knowing about its government is protected by
the guarantee of a free press, but the protection is indirect. The Constitution itself is neither a Freedom of Information Act nor an Official Secrets Act.

The Constitution, in other words, establishes the con-
test, not its resolution. Congress may provide a resolution,
at least in some instances, through carefully drawn legislation. For the rest, we must rely, as so often in our system
we must, on the tug and pull of the political forces in
American society.

Newspapers, television networks, and magazines have
sometimes been outrageously abusive, untruthful, arrogant,
and hypocritical. But it hardly follows that elimination of
a strong and independent press is the way to eliminate
abusiveness, untruth, arrogance, or hypocrisy from government itself.

It is quite possible to conceive of the survival of our

Republic without an autonomous press. For openness and honesty in government, for an adequate flow of information between the people and their representatives, for a sufficient check on autocracy and despotism, the traditional competition between the three branches of government, supplemented by vigorous political activity, might be enough.

The press could be relegated to the status of a public utility. The guarantee of free speech would presumably put some limitation on the regulation to which the press could be subjected. But if there were no guarantee of a free press, government could convert the communications media into a neutral "marketplace of ideas." Newspapers and television networks could then be required to promote contemporary government policy or current notions of social justice.

Such a constitution is possible; it might work reasonably well. But it is not the constitution the founders wrote. It is not the constitution that has carried us through nearly two centuries of national life. Perhaps our liberties might survive without an independent established press. But the founders doubted it, and, in the year 1974, I think we can all be thankful for their doubts.

Let me emphasize again what I tried to indicate at the beginning of this discussion. The First Amendment views that I have expressed are my own. I have not spoken for the Court, and particularly I have not spoken for Mr. Justice White. While he and I are in agreement about many things, we have also sometimes disagreed—from as long ago as 1939 to as recently as last Tuesday. And, whatever else we may have learned at this law school, I think each of us learned somewhere along the way that the person who disagrees with you is not necessarily wrong.

In my opening remarks I spoke of the law school that I knew as a student. But I am not here today in the role of an aging alumnus with wistful memories of the way things used to be. All of us are here not so much to commemorate a golden past as to celebrate the present, and to express our faith in a bright and solid future.

I spoke earlier of the distinguished members of the faculty who are gone. The fact is that many of the finest teachers of my day are still here, or only recently retired: Fleming James, Myres McDougal, J. W. Moore, Fred Rodell, Eugene Rostow. And the more important fact is that the law school through the years has been remarkably successful in its continuing program of faculty self-renewal—drawing here teachers and scholars of proven achievement or extraordinary promise. Of them all, I mention only the name of Alexander Bickel, not just because of his nationally recognized distinction, but because I am so sorry he cannot be with us today.

Among the students now here there are undoubtedly future judges and justices, perhaps future Senators and congressmen and governors and Cabinet officers, and maybe even a future President. But that is not what was really important about the Yale Law School of a generation ago, nor what is important now, nor what will be important in future years. The number of our graduates who have gone into government service is exceedingly high. But public service is surely not limited to government service. The real impact of the Yale Law School will always be most broadly felt through the leadership of its sons and daughters in countless other areas of professional and business activity.

Whatever place any of us may now occupy, all of us share one priceless experience in common. All of us have spent three of the most formative years of our lives in *this* place—challenged by the ideal of excellence, and prepared by that challenge to go forth from here with the will and the confidence to do our best with any task that life may bring.

The opportunity for that priceless experience at this great law school, for generations of young men and women yet to come, is surely worth preserving for *at least* another 150 years.

"THE NEGLECT OF THE SONG" [3]

J. William Fulbright [4]

On December 18, 1974, J. William Fulbright addressed a luncheon gathering of about 250 persons assembled in the Grand Ballroom of the National Press Club, in Washington, D.C. His listeners were mainly reporters, editors, writers, publishers, and others associated with publishing. The National Press Club regards itself as "a public forum for the great issues of the day; it is a tavern of good fellowship, a hearty restaurant, a quiet retreat, a busy trading post for reporters and their news sources." It has attracted as speakers Presidents, Senators, Representatives, and prime ministers and other foreign dignitaries, as well as journalists and authors. On occasion the club presents such popular personalities as Gloria Steinem, Muhammad Ali, and Leonard Bernstein.

According to Fulbright, the program chairman invited him to "reminisce a bit over" his "remarkable career in the Congress." The former Arkansas Senator, who was nearing the end of his fifth term in the Senate, was of considerable interest to those present because of his recent defeat by Dale Bumpers, the young governor of Arkansas, in the state's Democratic senatorial primary. Many had lamented the defeat of Fulbright because of the important role he had played in the Senate, particularly as chairman of the Foreign Relations Committee (since 1959). As Daniel Yergin reports, "Fulbright has been more important as a statesman-educator than as a great lawmaker," sponsoring little legislation, but holding many hearings to publicize the foreign policy of various Administrations (New York *Times Magazine,* November 24, 1974).

Fulbright's speech to the National Press Club is unusual because he levels criticism at those in the audience and at the press in general. Like others, journalists resent public censure. But investigative and advocacy reporting (the "new journalism"), made popular by exposés on Vietnam and Watergate, have resulted in ruthlessness or what Fulbright refers to as "a surge of moral extremism," or perhaps as a lack of "civility." Pointedly, the Senator says, "The media have acquired an undue preoccupation with the apprehension of wrongdoers, a fascination with the singer to the neglect of the song."

[3] Delivered to the National Press Club, Washington, D.C., December 18, 1974. Quoted by permission. Title supplied by editor.
[4] For biographical note, see Appendix.

With a trace of a soft Arkansas drawl, clear enunciation and a low, pleasant voice, he speaks at a slow rate. "His eyes, which are his most expressive feature, seem to reflect the mood of his speech." Wearing horn-rimmed glasses, he has a "friendly, engaging smile," is "erect but casual" (particularly when he is in Arkansas), moves very little, and uses few gestures (except a short jab with his removed glasses) while speaking. He has been accused of speaking "above the heads of the average audience" (Lera R. Kelly, *Southern Speech Journal*, Spring 1962, p 232–8).

Fulbright, concludes Yergin, "may well figure in history as the most famous Senator of his time, blemished, not necessarily a hero, but a man of perception and courage, a historic figure, a statesman." "A complicated man," he will be remembered as "the Great Dissenter."

I appreciate the Press Club inviting me to this luncheon in this last week of my thirty-two years in the Congress, and the week before Christmas.

What an appropriate time for us to be charitable to one another, just for the day—I do not mean that quite the way it may sound, for the press on the whole has been quite fair and considerate of me during these thirty-two years.

Mr. Prina, in his letter inviting me to this luncheon, suggested that I reminisce a bit over my "remarkable" career in the Congress. The words are his. The most remarkable thing to me is that I survived these thirty-two years! I have been both astonished and grateful to the electorate of Arkansas for giving me the opportunity for so many interesting experiences, experiences quite unlike those of any other activity with which I am acquainted.

One of the most pleasant experiences of this period was my friendship with Walter Lippmann. Shortly after Betty and I came to Washington in 1943, we met the Lippmanns and saw them frequently until they moved to New York in 1967.

Walter Lippmann was, as so many have attested during the past few days, the most perceptive and most lucid observer of the affairs of this world during this century. His books and his columns did so very much to inform, to educate, and I may add to civilize public opinion in our country. It was a great privilege and a pleasure to know so well such a fine human being—and, of course, I would not have known him but for my position in the Congress.

Eric Sevareid in last Sunday's *Post* wrote an excellent tribute to Lippmann under the title, "Truth Was His Love."

I expect that there are few people in this room or in the Congress who do not feel that they also are seekers of or expositors of the truth. In addition to this shared interest in seeking the truth, the press is such an important factor in the life of all public officials, especially members of Congress, that it seems appropriate to me to reminisce about the press for these few minutes at our disposal.

In recent years—the Vietnam and Watergate years—the American press has demonstrated its commitment to the Biblical injunction that "the truth shall make you free."

The unrestrained enthusiasm of the pursuit of this commitment by some segments of the press has raised some doubts in my mind about the validity of the proposition.

A number of crucial distinctions may be swept aside by an indiscriminate commitment to the truth—the distinction, for instance, between factual and philosophical truth, or between truth in the sense of factual disclosure and truth in the sense of insight. The latter, in my opinion, are higher forms of truth, more meaningful and also more useful to society, even though a general truth can seldom be stated without qualifications or exceptions.

There are also certain fictions—or "myths"—which experience has shown to be useful to mankind, and because they are useful, we pretend to believe them, giving them thereby a kind of metaphorical truth. One of these is the fiction that "the king can do no wrong." He can, of course —and he does, and everybody knows it. But in the course of many centuries of Anglo-Saxon constitutional evolution, it became apparent that it was useful to the cohesion and morale of society to attribute certain civic virtues to the chief of state, even when he patently lacked them. Properly understood, respect and confidence in the chief of state are not a literal fact but a metaphorical one, expressing the society's respect for and confidence in itself and in its institutions.

The "myth" is more easily utilized in a constitutional monarchy than in our presidential Republic, in which ceremonial and political powers are vested in the same individual. It can be done, however, and until fairly recently we have done it, according certain honors to the President as chief of state while holding him to political account in his role as head of government. We managed, at one and the same time, to tell ourselves that our ceremonial President was regally clad, while the political President might be naked as a jaybird.

It took a certain dexterity to sustain the fiction, but more important, it rested on a kind of social contract—an implicit agreement among Congress, the press and the people that some matters are better left undiscussed, not so as to suppress information, but in recognition, as a French writer put it, that "there are truths which can kill a nation." What he meant, I believe, was that there are gradations of truth in a society, and that there are some which are more significant than others and which may also be destructive. The self-confidence and cohesion of a society may be a fact, but it can be diluted or destroyed by other facts such as the corruption or criminality of the society's leaders. Something like that may have been what Voltaire had in mind when he wrote that "there are truths which are not for all men, nor for all times." Or as Mark Twain put it, even more cogently, "Truth is the most valuable thing we have. Let us economize it."

In the last decade—this Vietnam and Watergate decade —we have lost our ability to "economize" the truth. That Puritan self-righteousness which is never far below the surface of American life has broken through the frail barriers of civility and restraint, and the press has been in the vanguard of the new aggressiveness. I am not—let me state with all possible emphasis—advocating silence or suppression of criticism. I have not been particularly backward in that department myself, and I have no regrets for my maverick ways. What I do deplore—and that, too, with all possible emphasis—is the shifting of the attack from policies to personalities, from matters of tangible consequence to the nation as a whole to matters of personal morality of uncertain relevance to the national interest.

We used, it seems to me, to make this distinction, while also perpetuating the useful myth that "the king can do no wrong." One means we used was blaming someone else —in a ceremonial way. When I first publicly criticized the Johnson Administration, for example, over the Dominican intervention in 1965, I was at some pains to attribute the errors of judgment involved to the "President's advisers" and not to the President himself—although I can disclose to you today that I was not wholly free of doubts about the judgment of the top man. Our focus was different in those days: It was sometimes evident in hearings before the Foreign Relations Committee on Vietnam and other matters that facts were being withheld or misrepresented, but our concern was with the events and policies involved rather than with the individual officials who chose—or more often were sent—to misrepresent the Administration's position. Our concern was with correcting mistakes rather than punishing those who made them.

It is always a matter of relative emphasis, I admit. But since Watergate—and here my criticism is directed particularly to the press—the balance has shifted decisively. The media have acquired an undue preoccupation with the apprehension of wrongdoers, a fascination with the singer to the neglect of the song. The result is not only an excess of emphasis on personalities but short shrift for significant policy questions. I am not convinced, for example, that Watergate was as significant for the national interest as Mr. Nixon's extraordinary innovations in foreign policy.

The Nixon détente policy was by no means neglected, but it certainly took second place in the news to Watergate.

To take a matter close to my own domain, I was deeply disappointed by the media's neglect of the extensive hearings held by the Foreign Relations Committee earlier this year on the various aspects of détente—not, I assure you, because I hunger for personal publicity at this late date, but because the issues involved in détente are absolutely central to our foreign policy and even to our national survival. At the same time that the media were ignoring the détente hearings, they gave unlimited, to the point of tedium, coverage to the resignation and all related subjects.

One circumstance which probably contributed to this distortion of the more traditional balance of the press was the existence of the tapes, an unprecedented and dramatic kind of evidence of personal delinquency in high places. The tapes really did undress the king.

With the assistance of the tapes, the press has exposed the wrongdoers most effectively, but I believe at the same time you have neglected your higher responsibility of public education. With an exception or two such as the National Public Radio, the media convey only fragments of those public proceedings which are designed to inform the general public. A superstar can always command the attention of the press, even with a banality. An obscure professor can scarcely hope to, even with a striking idea, a new insight, or a lucid simplification of a complex issue. A bombastic accusation, a groundless prediction, or best of all a "leak," will usually gain a Senator his heart's content of publicity; a reasoned discourse, more often than not, is destined for entombment in the *Congressional Record*. A member of the Foreign Relations Committee staff suggested recently that the committee had made a mistake in holding the détente hearings in public; if we had held them in closed session, he observed, and leaked the transcripts, the press would have covered them generously.

The heart of the matter is a surge of moral extremism

in our attitude toward politics and political leaders. The genesis, I have no doubt, was Vietnam, followed by Watergate, both of which inevitably undercut confidence in our national leadership. Moral indignation, however, even *justified* moral indignation, has a tendency to become vindictive and self-righteous. Mistakes of judgment come to be perceived as premeditated malevolence, and an interest in correcting mistakes gives way to an obsession with punishing the malefactors, with giving them their just deserts.

My own view is that no one should get everything he deserves—the world would become a charnel house. Looking back on the Vietnam war, it never occurred to me that President Johnson was guilty of anything worse than bad judgment. He deceived the Congress, and he deceived me personally, over the Gulf of Tonkin episode in 1964 and his purposes in the election of '64. I resented that, and I am glad the deceit was exposed, but I never wished to carry the matter beyond exposure. I never had the slightest sympathy with those who called President Johnson and his advisers "war criminals."

We should stop conducting our affairs like a morality play. Lying and dirty tricks are intolerable not because of what they do to the trickster's soul but because they disrupt our society and its institutions. Because they do, it is essential that they be deterred, but this can usually be accomplished by exposure, embarrassment and censure; it does not require hunting down the malefactors to their utter ruin. An intolerance of lying can and should be reconciled with a degree of tolerance for liars—considering that few of us get through an ordinary day without trimming the truth once or twice.

In a democracy we ought to try to think of our public servants not as objects of adulation or of revilement, but as servants in the literal sense, to be lauded or censured, retained or dispensed with, according to the competence with which they do the job they were hired to do. Bitter disillusionment with our leaders is the other side of the coin of worshiping them. If we did not expect our leaders to be demigods, we would not be nearly as shocked by their failures and transgressions.

The media have a special responsibility for the restoration of civility in these matters, not only because they have contributed to the incivility, but also because there is no one to correct journalistic excesses except the members of the profession themselves. The media have become a fourth branch of government in every respect except for their immunity from checks and balances. This is as it should be—I can conceive of no restraints on the press which would not be worse than the excesses to which I have referred. But because you cannot and should not be restrained from outside, you have a special responsibility to restrain yourselves.

After a long era of divisiveness and acrimony, we are in need of a reaffirmation of the social contract among people, government and the media. The essence of that contract is a measure of voluntary restraint, an implicit agreement among the major groups and interests in our society that none will apply their powers to the fullest. For all the ingeniousness of our system of checks and balances, our ultimate protection against tyranny is the fact that we are a people who have not wished to tyrannize one another. "The republican form of government," wrote Herbert Spencer in 1891, "is the highest form of government: but because of this it requires the highest type of human nature—a type nowhere at present existing." We have shown in times of adversity in the past that we are capable of this "highest type of human nature." Let us call it into existence once again—we have never needed it more.

HIGHER EDUCATION

ALL OUR INSTITUTIONS ARE IN DISARRAY [1]

Robert M. Hutchins [2]

On May 20, 1974, Robert M. Hutchins spoke to the faculty, students, and invited guests of California State University at the dedication of the university's new Graduate Studies and Research Center in Long Beach. The center, completed April 11, 1974, was created to "foster dialogue and sense of community among graduate students and faculty, e.g., publications, informal and formal meetings, including regular colloquies for creative and scholarly presentations." Hutchins was a highly appropriate choice to address those assembled, for he has devoted his life to promoting dialogue among scholars and influential persons, first at the University of Chicago (1929–1951) and later as president of the Center for the Study of Democratic Institutions (1954–1974). At the Center, some of the greatest minds of the day engaged in thrice-weekly dialogues, discussing such key issues as environmental threats, poverty, aging, constitutional crises, and medical malpractice (New York *Times,* April 4, 1975). Expressing his approval of the new graduate center, Hutchins said:

> It is to the great credit of this university that it has established this center precisely to overcome the communicative disorders that now afflict us all. . . . But it is necessary . . . if we are to survive, that we understand one another. We must engage in a continuous dialogue designed to promote understanding.

The speech, reported to have been delivered extemporaneously, is loose in structure and anecdotal in content. Declaring that he was making his "last speech . . . on the subject of education," Hutchins reinforced his insistence upon humane or liberal education, a theme that he has advocated since his first days with Yale Law School some fifty years ago. (For an earlier speech by Hutchins on this subject, see REPRESENTATIVE AMERICAN SPEECHES: 1971–1972, p 161–71.) He states his message clearly when he defines

[1] Delivered at the dedication ceremony of California State University's Graduate Studies and Research Center, Long Beach, California, May 20, 1974. Appeared in *Center Report* (December, 1974, p 19-21), a publication of the Center for the Study of Democratic Institutions. Copyright © 1975, University of California/Long Beach. Quoted by permission.

[2] For biographical note, see Appendix.

liberal education as "the arts of communication and the arts of using the mind." He continues:

> They are the arts indispensable to further learning, for they are the arts of reading, writing, speaking, listening, figuring. They have a timeless quality, for they are indispensable no matter what happens in any state of the world. They are, in fact, the arts of becoming human.

Robert M. Hutchins is among the foremost American academic speakers of this century. Audiences have found him to be impressive and persuasive. If we can believe that this speech is his final one on education, it is a fitting valedictory for this educational reformer.

You will be glad to note and so will the whole educational world that this is the last speech I intend to make on the subject of education. I mention this because I well remember the first invitation I had to speak on education. I became secretary of Yale University on January 1, 1923, and on the afternoon of the next day I received an invitation to speak to the alumni at Montclair, New Jersey. I wrote the secretary of the Montclair Alumni Association and asked him what he wanted me to speak about. He said he didn't care what I spoke about as long as what I said was vivid, sympathetic and gutsy. This will give you some idea of what Yale University was like in those days, but it will also indicate why I have achieved that degree of frustration which is so manifest in all of these years to be vivid, sympathetic and gutsy, and I have failed. I shall make no effort, I hasten to assure you, to be any of these things tonight.

Many years ago, the Oxford Union adopted by a very large majority, the following motion: "Columbus went too far." I don't think we can blame it on Columbus. All our institutions are in disarray and we're becoming worried for the first time in a long time even about our ability to finance our governmental operations.

In studying the curriculum of this university, the California Studies and Research Center, California State University at Long Beach, to which I've devoted a great deal of attention, I have observed with interest that it is possible to obtain here a degree of Master of Arts in communicative disorders. I should have thought no special degree of this kind was necessary. All graduates of all American universities must be masters of communicative disorders because their training makes it impossible for them to communicate with anybody outside their own fields. Departmentalization, specialization, fragmentation, plus that striking example of Yankee ingenuity, the credit system—these have all produced communicative disorders so pervasive that they may be said to be the dominant characteristic of our institutions of higher learning today.

It is to the great credit of this university that it has established this center precisely to overcome the communicative disorders that now afflict us all. I have to say though that I think these disorders are of the most far-reaching and disturbing consequences. It is not necessary for the people of this country or for the world to agree upon anything or to agree with one another. That would be too much to expect and it might turn out to be very boring. But it is necessary, I think, if we are to survive, that we understand one another. We must engage in a continuous dialogue designed to promote understanding. At the moment it would be very difficult to say (and, in fact, I haven't heard anybody say it) that we have a political community in this country. We can't communicate with one another.

A common educational program once thought indispensable has disappeared and over the last five years many books have received much acclaim for recommending that our public schools be abolished. They have shown not the slightest interest in the consequences of such action on the formation or maintenance of the political community. Their interest has been in gratifying the whims of individuals which leads to the kind of amoral egotism disclosed, for example, by the Watergate transcripts.

I take it that the basic requirement for the formation of a political community is a common liberal education, an education that is appropriate to a community of free men. This has nothing to do with vocational training or with what is now called career education, whatever that may mean. The liberal arts are the arts of communication and the arts of using the mind. They are the arts indispensable to further learning, for they are the arts of reading, writing, speaking, listening, figuring. They have a timeless quality, for they are indispensable no matter what happens in any state of the world. They are, in fact, the arts of becoming human. The object of liberal or basic education may be said to be the transformation of young animals into human beings. I believe in liberal education for everybody and I have never seen any evidence that it is beyond the reach of everybody. Nor have I ever seen any evidence that educational institutions are incapable of imparting it if they will. I hasten to say that they don't impart it. When I was teaching in the Yale Law School many years ago, it seemed to me that the principal handicap under which we labored was the necessity of teaching these carefully selected college graduates what they could have learned at the age of six, or possibly four. After all, if you study law you have to know how to read and write.

In any practical activity, purpose is the guiding principle. Purpose is a principle of allocation. It tells you what to work on. But more important, purpose is a principle of limitation. It tells you what not to work on. The miscellaneous and heterogeneous character of institutions of learning from kindergarten up in this country, shows that we don't know what we are trying to do.

I became an administrative officer on January 1, 1923, and for more than fifty-one years, therefore, I have seen educational institutions from the kindergarten up settle their programs by logrolling, by public relations, by political pressure and most of all by asking where the money is. I hate to tell you that I have met with committees of great universities to discuss education and research and I have found them talking about those mystic initials ADA and FTE, average daily attendance, and full-time equivalents, and this is what they wanted to talk about because manipulating these letters produce the revenue, through a kind of mystical algebra, derived from the state. What this led to was public relations as the determinant of policy. We tried to think of courses that would attract students and it mattered not whether these courses had any intellectual content.

I admit to a prejudice that in many places is regarded as indefensible. I do believe that educational programs and every course in an educational program should at least make an effort to have intellectual content. I would go further in my wilder moments and say that, if an educational program or if a course in an educational program had no intellectual content, it should be abolished. In these meetings that I had with the representatives of great universities there was a general fear expressed that courses with intellectual content would for that very reason alone frighten students and hence defeat the purpose the university had in view. This definition of purpose would thus amount to saying this, "It would be getting money for things not worth doing." This shows the failure of purpose as a principle of limitation; the number of things a university can do that are not worth doing is, I assure you, limitless.

If you want a single example, one I fear, with which I am too much identified, I would suggest that the popularity of big-time, intercollegiate football shows there is no relationship or no necessary relationship between the value of what you're doing and the public esteem in which you bask because of doing it.

I should like to lay before you a simple proposition, that the purpose of the educational system as a whole is to form and maintain the political community and to equip the citizen (I emphasize the word citizen because citizens are what we seem to lack), with the means of going on learning all his life. This is an enormous task. And the job of educational leaders is not to think up educational gimmicks that will deceive the public into supporting things not worth doing, but to explain to the people what education is, why it is important, why it is as important as the Founding Fathers thought, and even more, why in a technological age the rapidity of change makes current fads the least effective of all educational programs.

The trouble with current fads is that they won't stay current.

So much for the purpose of education in general and basic education in particular. I would now like to lay before you the proposition that the purpose of a university is understanding. At the Yale Law School, what in the world could we think we were doing when we tried to teach the students how to manipulate the rules in order to get rich at the New York bar? We were a university after all. We said we were a university. We told the students we were a university. We told them they would get a university education. We never confided to them our true secret, which was, that we were a trade school.

Now the law is a dazzling panorama of the world showing what is happening to society and in particular, what is happening to two basic American values, freedom and justice. To understand the law is to understand the stage of civilization mankind has reached and to have some faint notion about how it might advance to a higher stage.

Half the faculty of the Yale Law School felt that the way to teach law was to teach a boy to draw a will which he could learn much faster in a law office. They thought what we should do was to teach the current rules of procedure which could have been learned much faster under supervision in court. In any event, in the law, as in everything else, change is the order of the day. I'm sorry to have to tell you that it is only a slight exaggeration to say that everything I studied in law school, and what is worse, everything I taught there, has now been overruled or repealed.

I sometimes think of those aging law students of mine, now sixty or more years old, wandering around the streets of New York trying to figure out what happened. Did I lie to them? No, I don't think I consciously lied to them. What I did was to tell them what the law was, and, as of the date on which I told them, I think I was substantially correct. But as of the date on which they had to put it into practice, I was overwhelmingly wrong. The reception accorded the Warren Court was a perfect example of what I mean. The bar as a whole in the United States could not understand the Warren Court because it couldn't understand the United States. There was never any way in which my students at the Yale Law School could come to understand the United States because we never mentioned the matter.

I used to teach the law of evidence, a very moving subject. Somebody ought to make a motion picture out of it. There were two rules that absolutely fascinated me. You know that the hearsay rule, which is the principal rule of the law of evidence, requires that the witness should be present under oath and subject to cross-examination, or his testimony is inadmissible, with certain exceptions. Those exceptions are supposed to be substitutes for a guarantee of truth comparable with the oath and cross-examination. For example: if as you fall dead, you say "Hutchins shot me," this is admissible at my trial because the fear of death that was present in your mind and worse, the fear of meeting your Maker which was present in your mind, was a guarantee of the truth of your observations. You'll notice that this has little to do with the United States or its institutions.

There is a rule in the law of evidence that flight from the scene of a crime is evidence of consciousness of guilt. This one I traced back by that painful research which characterizes the activities of all law professors to that sentence in the Bible which says, "The wicked flee when no man pursueth and the righteous are as bold as a lion." Whether this applies to the American righteous, whether there are American righteous, one does not really learn from this slogan. But it is very useful because it is so easy to remember, and the question is sure to come up on the bar examination.

Well, I said that everything I taught at the Yale Law School had been overruled or repealed; but the process still goes on. The Burger Court is now busy overruling or modifying much of what had been overruled or modified since my day. For example: the great rule of *Miranda* versus *Arizona* which was one of the triumphs of the Warren Court, which provides for the regulation of questions addressed to a prisoner in custody, has now been, for all practical purposes, largely modified. And this process will continue. I believe it will continue at a rate considerably accelerated if the present incumbent remains in the White House. The result will be that all the magnificent instruction in what the law is, which will by this time be the law as handed down by the Warren Court, will be totally useless to those neophytes at the bar who have graduated from the most prestigious law schools with the highest grades.

To teach the rules, therefore, is as much a waste of time now as it was when I was doing it. To understand the law is even more important than it was then because all our legal institutions are in disarray.

Now we come to the real question: "How does one understand the law as distinguished from simply memorizing the rules that courts and legislatures have laid down?" If we could answer this question, we might discover the purpose of all graduate study. I have to say at the outset that I cannot reconcile myself to the notion that the purpose of graduate study any more than the purpose of undergraduate study is to get a credential, a certificate, a diploma, or a degree that will satisfy an employer and expedite the labors of a personnel officer, that will lead to a better job, or that will give one a leg up the social ladder. I cannot find any way of reconciling this position with any rational, defensible conception of education at any level. I suggest, on the contrary, that credentialism is the curse of American education. We should award all educational credentials to all Americans at birth. If we could do this, then we could get on with education.

The way to understand the law and I mention the law so often only because I know you do not teach it here, the way to understand the law and the way to understand any other subject is to understand it in its context, in its relations to all other subjects that bear upon it. In the case of the law, philosophy, history, psychology, and all the social sciences bear upon it, and it bears on all of them, and I venture to suggest that it is this, this centrality, this intellectual centrality, this bearing that the law has on all intellectual subjects and the bearing that they have on it, it is this that makes the law a university subject. If the law is not taught this way, then there is no reason why it should not be relegated to trade schools and I mean trade schools that are admittedly trade schools in name as well as in fact.

If the object of a law school were to teach the rules nobody else in the university could or should be interested in it. Who cares? The law school, like most law schools today would have the same heating plant and the same president as the rest of the university, but like most law schools today, it would have little intellectual connection with the rest of the university.

Here I suggest that any section of the university that cannot have an intellectual connection with the rest of the university has no place in the university and should be abolished. Since all other disciplines in the university today are in the same shape that the law is in and since a university does not exist in my opinion unless it is an intellectual community, it follows that almost no universities exist in the United States for almost none of them is or can be an intellectual community.

In fact, I have heard it said in the highest quarters, namely in Berkeley, that the idea of an intellectual community is no longer possible, that it is, in fact, dangerous and misleading. We are here, they say in Berkeley, or some of them say in Berkeley, as a group of technical schools teaching people to do research and to teach in university departments like our own. This overlooks the losses that go with the loss of the intellectual community. I am prepared to assert that no university discipline either in teaching or research can flourish by itself or can even grasp what it is doing in the absence of a common liberal education and an intellectual community in which liberal education and advanced study based on liberal education are carried on. If the object of a university is understanding, these requirements must be met. Specialization, in other words, if it is to succeed on its own terms, must rest on liberal education and it must be illuminated by the light of other disciplines in the intellectual community.

THE VITAL UNIVERSITY [3]

JAMES H. McBATH [4]

"Higher education is in the throes of one of its greatest periods of transition," concluded the Carnegie Council for Policy Studies in Higher Education. A panel of educational leaders forecast "that financial pressure would probably compel one of every ten colleges and universities in the United States to merge, consolidate, or close down entirely within the next five years" (New York *Times*, April 16, 1975).

From many sides institutions of higher learning are under fire. Rapidly mounting costs, increased competition for the tax dollar, extravagant use of available resources, oversupply of graduates with higher degrees, and changes in the mores of students have brought collegiate education, both public and private, under rigid scrutiny. Particularly among private institutions, tuition and other fees have increased so rapidly that even middle-class families with substantial incomes are having difficulty keeping children in school. Reliance on behavioral objectives, career education, greater centralization of governing authority, the determination of allotments on the basis of enrollment (FTE, i.e. full time equivalent), and unionization of faculties all threaten what has been known as liberal education.

Fully aware of these pressures, James H. McBath, chairman of the Department of Speech Communication at the University of Southern California, faced several hundred persons at the 1974 initiation ceremonies of the Phi Kappa Phi honor society. The audience was composed of about fifty initiates, their families and friends, members of the faculty, and school officials. Dr. McBath, the featured speaker at the initiation, has written that he

used the occasion to discuss . . . the central problem of higher education today—preservation of the integrity of the university when commercial criteria are used in academic decision making. The speech was meant to challenge the factory model of the managerial revolution and to reaffirm the essential and unique character of the university.

In many ways this address is a model of good speech composition. The introduction, the problem, the solution, and the

[3] Delivered at the Phi Kappa Phi annual initiation ceremonies, Hancock Auditorium, University of Southern California, Los Angeles, June 5, 1975. Printed in *Phi Kappa Phi Journal*, Fall 1974, p 54-9. Quoted by permission.

[4] For biographical note, see Appendix.

127

appeal for acceptance are clearly discernible. He has filled his speech with apt quotations, facts, and statistics. He demonstrates that he carefully assembled his materials and put them in a polished form. His sources appealed to his intellectual listeners.

Dr. McBath is a forceful and effective speaker. His erect bearing, directness, pleasant voice and good smile radiate his enthusiasm and add to his persuasiveness. A well-read student of argumentation and rhetoric, he was a high school and college debater and has taught graduate courses in public address.

It was Samuel Johnson who reflected on occasions such as this: "That academical honours, or any others, should be conferred with exact proportion to merit, is more than human judgement or human integrity have given reason to expect." Still I think it fair to say that the four-year winnowing process you have survived in gaining Phi Kappa Phi membership makes credible your entitlement to this recognition. Your efforts should, at this late hour, at least entitle you to respite from talks from teachers; but custom condemns you to occasions such as baccalaureate, commencement, and welcomes into honor societies.

You are leaving college at a time when another great debate about universities is under way. "If the number of commission reports on higher education is any index," remarked Clark Kerr, "concern for the subject has been increasing almost logarithmically since the 1940s." During the first four years of this decade, no fewer than six groups have published their final conclusions and recommendations. Occupying central attention, of course, is the Carnegie Commission on Higher Education, whose 21 special studies and series of 80 sponsored research reports make its work the most extensive study of higher education ever undertaken. Now available as well are findings of the Newman Task Forces, the National Board on Graduate Education, and the Panel on Alternate Approaches to Graduate Education. Such an array of documents and recommendations almost intimidates anyone venturing the selection of a few ideas for brief discussion. There are, however, several emergent questions that confront all of higher education but have special relevancy to independent higher education.

As a starting point let us bluntly acknowledge a single fact: The American university is facing a financial crisis unparalleled in its history. Instruction costs, building costs, maintenance costs, and overall inflation are soaring. Tuition, at least at most universities, has about reached its practical ceiling; tuition is near the limit of its ability to increase income without repelling tuition payers. This problem annually confronts students who are asked to pay a never-ending increase in tuition and faculty who are asked to teach more and better while earning comparatively less. During the past ten years, the tuition at member schools of the Association of American Universities has increased substantially, while real faculty income at the same institutions over this period has declined.

Faced with mounting costs, diminishing resources, and self-defeating tuition increases, higher education began learning a new vocabulary. "If we could discover the little backstairs door that for any age serves as the secret entranceway to knowledge," said historian Carl Becker, "we will do well to look for certain unobtrusive words with uncertain meanings that are permitted to slip off the tongue or the pen without fear and without research; words which, having from constant repetition lost their metaphorical significance, are unconsciously mistaken for objective realities." According to Becker, in the thirteenth century the key words would no doubt have been: sin, grace, salvation, and heaven; in the eighteenth century such words would have been: natural law, first cause, reason, humanity, and perfectibility; in the nineteenth century: matter, fact, evolution, progress; and in the early twentieth century: relativity, process, adjustment, and complex. More recently we have responded to student rights, black power, multiversity, and relevance. During the seventies, the little backstairs doors that confront us in higher education are cost effectiveness, systems management, computerized campus, productivity, fixed-term renewable contracts, and account-ability.

To the university system, beset with financial problems, the impulse to apply the industrial model was irresistible. By 1966 Francis Rourke and Glenn Brooks were able to publish a work proclaiming, as its title did, *The Managerial Revolution in Higher Education*. While you have been in college the issue of the university as academy or as business has become central. To the new managers the university is just another large system. It has raw material (students), a labor force (faculty and support personnel), instruments of production (classroom, laboratories, libraries), a production schedule (academic requirements, classes admitted, and classes graduated), management (the trustees and central administration), and a production index (the cost of producing a student credit hour). In this view, faculty are workers, producing quietly, unobtrusively, on schedule, their "fair share" of the units of production. The product (students) reflects "value added" in manufacture. The cheerful assumption is that more has been put into students' heads than has been taken out.

The managerial revolution reached its full glory several years ago in—of all places—Fairfield, Iowa, where a small college was turned into a financial triumph and a national scandal. James Koerner tells the story in his book, *The Parsons College Bubble:*

Can you run a college like a business? Can you give economic considerations first priority in making academic decisions? Can you apply the principles of cost accounting to the instructional program? Can you put the curriculum on a production line? Can you get college professors to agree that "productivity" is something they ought to worry about and that their personal productivity, meaning the number of students they teach, should be measured? Can you suppress the faculty's normal preoccupation with its rights and privileges to the point that the institution's president can direct the institution's affairs like the chief executive of a major corporation? Can you inject free enterprise, the profit motive in particular, into higher education? And if you do, can you make a profit?

Yes, you might make a profit for a while. (Parsons of course is now defunct.) But you will ignore the complexity and richness of the university experience.

Give an unequivocal rating to every class you had during the past four years, not forgetting that the larger the class, the higher the rating. Award another rating to the counselors or advisers you met over this period. Give another number, to the informal advice received in dozens of unscheduled occasions with a variety of teachers. Can you assign numbers to the university administrators? According to the canons of accountability, you should be so able. Put a percentage on the encouragement you received at unexpected but important moments in your university career. Compute the contributions made by the library, guest lecturers, discussions with faculty members, participation in research projects, extracurricular activities, or a teaching assistant who finally made sense of the subject. All these, and more, make up your experience at this university. Impossible to quantify, you say. Of course, you are right. Education is not measured by corporate criteria.

Critics of the managerial revolution point out, as did Robert Hutchins several years ago, "that to analogize the trustees to the board of directors, the professors to employees, and the university president to the executive is to misconceive the nature, misstate the purpose, and pervert the spirit of the academic community." Contemporary leaders in higher education are equally critical of the analogy of factory and university. President Harold Enarson of Ohio State University recently said,

In my considered judgment, the managerial revolution creates the exact reverse of the goals that are sought. The impact of multiple sources of regulation on the university is to discourage flexibility, cripple initiative, dilute responsibility, and ultimately destroy true accountability. For the most part, the managerial revolution has meant the triumph of technique over purpose.

And Father Paul Reinert, chancellor of Saint Louis University, adds:

We must keep in mind when grappling with the fiscal quandary of higher education that there are substantive differences between a college and a business. Drive a corporation to the wall and it may make adjustments in its operations that enable it to bounce back; drive a college to the wall and you kill it.

Those schools that will best survive the seventies will display characteristics of the vital university.

(1) They will be themselves. That is they will forget about doing what the schools they admire are doing. The impulse to emulate some other institution—usually distant and often ivy-covered—causes many schools to overlook what they can do best. Often this impulse leads to a misallocation of resources since it is prohibitively expensive to purchase national leadership. Rather, these schools should seek out those areas of promise where modest financial support can produce the most striking results. The future of a university —perhaps this university—might well be in the newer disciplines or in nontraditional fields of learning. Playing the old-fashioned ratings game with other institutions is hazardous and imprudent.

Recently the Panel on Alternate Approaches to Graduate Education criticized the practice of periodically referring all of contemporary education to a single traditional norm. This practice, seen in reports of the American Council on Education, merely "endorses yesterday"; pioneering departments, newer disciplines, innovative programs are simply not listed. Thus, concludes the panel,

The models of university reality that are acknowledged are those whose shape was firm in 1920. And the places perceived as "distinguished" are, more often than not, those whose forms and ambience—from the commons rooms to the gothic gates to the occasionally embarrassing pride in "highly selective admissions policies"—imitate those of institutions founded in the world of kings and mass illiteracy.

(2) The more successful institutions will encourage maximum student and faculty involvement in processes of academic decision making. This will be done not just because it

is right, but because it will improve the quality of the institution. Warren Bennis, writing in *The Leaning Ivory Tower,* offers a guideline "so basic that it might well come first: Remember that change is most successful when those who are affected are involved in the planning." Bennis, now president of the University of Cincinnati, recounts his experience at Buffalo:

Nothing makes persons as resistant to new ideas or approaches as the feeling that change is being imposed upon them. The members of a university are unusually sensitive to individual prerogatives and to the administration's utter dependence on their support. Buffalo's academic plan was not popularly generated. Students and faculty did not contribute to its formulation. People resist change, even of a kind they basically agree with, if they are not significantly involved in the planning.

Though their approaches will vary widely, successful institutions of the seventies will learn the ways of maximizing collegiality, evolving more humane internal legal structures and a more realistic involvement of both faculty members and students in governance of the institution where they spend important years of their lives. It is no accident that there is a positive correlation between the academic quality of colleges and shared authority.

(3) These schools will encourage internal communication and criticism. The American university probably presents one of the most complex systems of human communication imaginable yet its success ultimately depends on the quality of its communication. Usually the product of decision making is seen only when finally phrased in a simple statement: "The university this morning announced its policy on . . ." But into that announcement has gone a complicated pattern of meetings, disagreements, conversations, personalities, negotiations, concessions, misunderstandings, and frequent differences of opinion. As far as I know there has never been a full-blown communication audit of any university; the project ought to be undertaken. We need to know the communication networks of a univer-

sity, the comparative effectiveness of different media and forms, the patterns of information acquisition and dissemination, the mythologies, perceptions, and symbols that impair or facilitate communication. We need to understand that criticism is not disloyalty, that ideas are best tested in debate, and that intelligent men and women may hold different opinions. Leisure World, not the university, is an island of tranquillity. "The noncontroversial university," noted Whitney Griswold, "is a contradiction in terms."

At this point you might expect some conventional expressions of doubt about the prospects of higher education. I have no doubts. Higher education continues to strengthen its place in American life. The demand for expertise varies widely, within fields, within narrow bands of time. Within the culture as a whole the course of that demand has been upward throughout the century, and both technological and social trends suggest an increasing need for specialized intelligence in the future.

Alexander Meiklejohn, when president of Amherst, wrote to members of the class of 1919:

> When a man chooses to go to college he declares that he wants to be different, that he is not satisfied to be what he is.
>
> If any one of you is satisfied with himself, he had better go back and keep still for fear something may happen to disturb his perfection.
>
> If those who stay are rightly dissatisfied with themselves, they will satisfy us.

To the Phi Kappa Phi initiates today may I say: "We are glad you stayed."

DEMOCRATIC LIVING: ASPIRATIONS AND ACHIEVEMENTS

"GIVEN TIME WE'LL GET IT TOGETHER" [1]

DANIEL JAMES, JR. [2]

Seldom is a speaker so powerful as a symbol that by his presence he becomes a main force in his persuasiveness. Ex-football player, fighter pilot, and highest ranking black officer in the Air Force, Lieutenant General Daniel James, Jr., has an image of this dimension. When he talks about Americanism, prejudice, and racial harmony, he is a living example of the message he wishes to communicate. He confirms Aristotle's observation that ethos (moral nature) "is the most potent of all means to persuasion" (*Rhetoric*, 1:2).

On February 14, 1975, Daniel ("Chappie") James, Jr. was the featured speaker for Black History Week at Escambia High School, in Pensacola, Florida. Having spoken the year before to the ninth and tenth grades, he now returned to address approximately 1,400 eleventh and twelfth graders. The school is a predominantly white high school (about 250 out of 4,000 are black). The general was of particular interest to the students in Pensacola because he is a native of the city (the youngest of a family of seventeen and a graduate of Washington High School across town.

This talk is an excellent one from many points of view. The reader should notice how General James keeps before his listeners his proposition: "And that's what we should be about, getting it together." Stated in popular language, the theme is meaningful to his listeners. He restates it at least twenty times, sometimes in different words but always implying his message by words and phrases such as "get it together"; "togetherness, pride, yes; hatred, separatism, never"; and "make sure your hand is stretched out there." Through his language and his use of colloquial expressions ("slide that in," "cast out some old hang-ups," "copped out," "getting it together," and "I've got news for you"), the speaker

[1] Delivered as a part of Black History Week at Escambia High School, Pensacola, Florida, February 14, 1975. Reprinted in the Pensacola *Journal*, February 15, 1975, and included in the *Congressional Record*, March 6, 1975. Quoted by permission. On July 1, 1975, James was nominated by President Ford to be a full general.

[2] For biographical note, see Appendix.

established rapport with his youthful listeners. His physical appearance, too, is commanding—he is six feet four inches tall and weighs 230 pounds.

General James is widely known for his speeches on patriotism and Americanism and has gained considerable attention for these talks in national and international publications. In 1967 and 1968 he received the George Washington Freedoms Foundation Medal. In 1970, when he received the Arnold Air Society Eugene M. Zucker Award, his citation read: ". . . fighter pilot with a magnificent record, public speaker, and eloquent spokesman for the American dream we so rarely achieve."

It's always a pleasure to come home; especially to come home to that kind of reception from my fellow Pensacolans.

It is fitting that I should return here a year later after having spoken to the other half of Escambia High School. It is remarkable that knowing that I'm a Washington High alumnus that you'd ask me back here because I understand that when you folks meet on the basketball court it's quite a scrimmage out there, but then, we always beat everybody in town anyway so nothing's changed. I had to slide that in.

But I come to you at a time when we are commemorating a gain. A week where we stop to take stock of a certain segment of history.

A young lady who sat here changed it, took a paragraph out of my speech and she hadn't even seen my speech. But it is exactly what I was going to express—that these things that are colored different shades of black or white or red or gray will pass with time and understanding of the various races of this great melting pot that is the United States of America.

As people reach out to one another and I, like she, I look forward to that great day when Black History Week will just become a part of American history week. And that will be its name, American History Week, where we take special time to look at the whole of what we are and where we came from.

Now we have various things, various songs, various poems, various art, figments of art, other parts of our culture that will be preserved as coming from the days when things were not really quite all right, but they will be used for just what they were intended, to mark those times.

And so we can assess the progress that we've made from back there to right here. The songs that we sang many times when I was in school here had a central chorus that really remarked on history and it was known as the Negro national hymn.

And it said

stony the road we trod, bitter the chastening rod felt in the days when hope unborn had died; yet with the steady beat had not our weary feet come to the place for which our fathers sighed? We have come over a way that with tears has been watered, we have come treading our path through the blood of the slaughtered, out of the gloomy past till now we stand at last where the white gleam of our bright star is cast.

Now that song was written over a hundred years ago, and even at that time black people in this country were assessing the progress that they had made since the days of bondage and slavery and they said we have come to the place "where the white gleam of our bright star is cast" and they were not indeed anywhere near where they are today and where they can go tomorrow, if we proceed to that place together, all of us, not looking for black achievement or white achievement or red achievement but American progress, the kind that has a chance only in our country and countries like ours but in our country to the greatest degree of all.

To get there, though, we've got to cast out some old hang-ups. We've got to be big enough no matter what our color to take the lead in making sure that that progress doesn't get staggered or slowed by retreats back to that path in the blood of the slaughtered.

We have marched enough, we have said enough, we have set out, we have walked out, we have copped out, we've sat in, the tune is go get it together.

You kids used to sing a song that I thought was very

hopeful. It said, "It's going to take a little more time to get it together." There's been a whole lot of people been working to get it together, like you and me, we're determined that every man and woman is going to be free but it's just going to take a little more time to get it together.

And that's what we should be about, getting it together. Do not fall into the tracks of our elders who still practice their biases. You indeed will inherit this earth. The meek will not inherit this earth, unfortunately or fortunately, because this earth is governed by the strong, not only the strong physically, but the strong morally and mentally who are willing to put down that bias, that bias of hatred based on race, creed, religion, social arts and the what-else-have-you.

Stop finding so many ways to hate each other because of race, creed, religion, social structure, section of the block, political party, falling on somebody else's scandal and picking at the bones of the fallen.

Get it together. That's the only way to move mountains. You, the young people of Pensacola, will inherit this land and the positions of leadership in it.

There are possibilities now for young black people to go that were never possible during my time except for the few of us who had the courage and the preparation and the guidance that I fortunately was given by my mother, who told me some of the things that I'm telling you today, who in spite of the serious biases that existed in that day fought our way to the top by building what she called the greatest weapon on earth and the greatest power on earth.

She said, "My son, don't you dare sacrifice your ability on the dubious altar of despair. You take advantage of every opportunity that's offered you right here in this town, in Pensacola, Florida, in the Deep South," where the benches were labeled "colored" and "white" in the parks at that time and the latrine doors "colored" and "white" and the buses "white—colored to the rear."

All of those signs that gave a built-in inferiority complex to young black lads growing up.

She said:

Don't pay any attention to that now. Because those will be later removed as a by-product of what you achieve and don't you make a profession of being black. You take advantage of every opportunity that's offered to you and build for yourself the greatest power on earth.

The power is called the power of excellence, and that's the only power worth investing in, the power of your own individual excellence, and you develop it. And you display it, and you use it to vault yourself to the top of your chosen field whatever it is, because you'll find that the power of excellence is a staple that doesn't decrease in value and it's in demand throughout the world and nobody questions its color.

And she was right. Nobody does question its color. And I entered the Air Force feeling that I was going to shoot for the top and I was going to try to be the greatest in my field, to vault with my power of excellence to the top of my chosen field because she said when you get up there with authority, you can do more to solve the ills that beset your people.

And you can't rise from the bottom with a brick or a torch or a harsh sign led on by some idiot who wants to make a profession of racism.

She was right—and I listened to her and I'm at the top of my field.

When I came into the Air Force I was determined to be a general officer and a leader of men, all men, not just black men, Americans, and I've got news for you—I am.

It is possible only here that these barriers have fallen as fast as they have. You can't stand there banging on that door of opportunity yelling, "Let me in! Let me in! Let me in!"

And all of a sudden, somebody opens that door and you say, "Wait a minute, I've got to go get bags." You stand there armed with your bags of knowledge and your bags of intelligence and your bags of tolerance and your bags of understanding and your bags of Americanism and when they crack that door you walk in and take charge and that's possible for anybody in this room at the sound of my voice here.

Don't trip on the stumbling blocks of reverse racism. I say to my young black friends, "Reach out your hands." There are a lot of hands out there reaching out to you in friendship and in help and many of these hands are white, but they find it pretty hard to grasp ahold if your hand is balled tightly into a fist of hate.

Togetherness, pride, yes. Hatred, separatism, never.

Bigotry is ugly no matter what its color, no matter from which direction it's beamed. The human dignity of a person must be respected and we must always remember that our race ends where another man or woman's begins. And we must practice that.

And I say to my young black friends all over the world to reach out because the opportunity is more equal now and it's going to be even more equal as we go along that those hands will be stretched out there and that that hand of friendship might be any color.

And I tell the white majority in the same voice, don't you make me a liar. Make sure your hand is stretched out there, because that's the only way we can go about it: with the strength that would make it possible for us to study war no more. Because if we have that internal strength that is born of togetherness, nobody will dare attack our nation.

Our internal strength is a bargaining chip that we must have in the international family of nations. So I ask you today to reach out to each other, not just during Black History Week, not just on "I Am an American Day" but every day. Get it together.

Make sure that you invest in the biggest weapon we have ever had in our arsenal.

Now this isn't a physical weapon, mind you, it's a psychological one. It's a weapon called unity. Unity in the principles of democracy of the law and the letter of the Constitution of the United States of America.

That is the greatest piece of paper in the world and the

words are great. You just have to make sure they work. It's up to you. You are the back that must provide the up-to-date modification of that weapon called unity.

We've come a long way in Pensacola. Assess that progress that black kids don't have to walk two and a half miles all the way across town to an all-black school anymore in this town.

There are no segregated public schools in this city. I'm proud to see. And we have solved most of the problems: those benches in the park are now painted green like the grass. And all of the citizens of my town sit on them and discuss other ways to improve it, I hope. We don't bother to get hung up, I hope, on little arguments that recall the evils of the past. When we get down to the point that all we've got to worry about is the flag and the song, then I think we've got it mostly whipped.

There was a lot more wrong with it when I was here. Long time ago. Let's not go back there. Over something as stupid and minor as a song, or a flag.

I want to tell you something that's ironic. When I was in the Philippines I went to the first all-white squadron that I was ever in because that's when we integrated the Air Force. And I made light of this and all of the rest of the members of my flight were white and the former flight leader was from Texas. And the symbol of our flight was the rebel flag. And we sang "Dixie" in the club every Friday night. And when I took over the flight they said "Well, Chappie, I guess you want to change that symbol. We'll get our razor blades out and scrape it off ourselves."

For what? I am from Dixie and I sang "Dixie" just as loud as anybody else and we defused the whole thing because the connotation of what some people were putting on "Dixie" ceased to be the connotation. It did not represent racial hatred, it represented our rallying cry, of what we were all about and we were indeed Americans, no matter what our color.

Now I will admit to you of all colors and races in here,

that there are some people who cannot stand progress and truths and a call for unity, but I ask you to assume the kind of dignity and the kind of attitude that you will be brave enough to not only make constructive change but to be a part of it and when the hang-up gets to be something non-remarkable that you will resist that by being an American first and everything else secondary.

And so I ask you to by the way you live your daily lives build for yourselves your link in that chain that is the unity that has always preceded the States of America, the United States of America, and make her strong and show that unity to the world and they won't stand against us and maybe they will listen to us when we say we don't want to study war no more.

And maybe they'll stand with us as we try to reach out to each other and get it altogether and then, and only then, standing together as Americans all, we'll all truly overcome.

"ASPIRATIONS . . . UNREQUITED" [3]

Yvonne B. Burke [4]

On March 10, 1975, Representative Yvonne B. Burke (Democrat, California) delivered the keynote address at the 1975 ceremony honoring the ten distinguished women selected to receive the Los Angeles *Times'* Women of the Year Awards. Ms. Burke was one of the honorees. Her audience included five hundred women gathered at the Times Mirror Building.

The speech is an excellent statement concerning the aspirations and accomplishments of women today. Dramatically she states her theme:

> It is a tragic irony that we despair over deprivations about to be suffered, while seven and one half million able and creative Americans sit idle, their collective energy languishing. . . .
>
> And women will be called upon as never before. As a group they possess the largest reservoir of unused capacity, for they have been unemployed and underemployed more than the rest.

Yvonne B. Burke, the first black woman ever elected to the California Assembly and the first woman to represent California in Congress in twenty years, came to national attention when she cochaired the 1972 Democratic Convention in Miami. *Time* magazine called her "an articulate advocate of consumer and environmental protection, women's and minority rights" (July 15, 1974, p 40). Forthright and direct, Ms. Burke is an excellent speaker.

Mr. Otis Chandler, Mrs. Dorothy Chandler, members of the Los Angeles *Times,* and distinguished guests: "The full and complete development of the world and the cause of peace require the maximum participation of women as well as men in all fields."

This statement, from the Preamble of the United Nations Declaration of the Elimination of Discrimination

[3] Delivered at the Women of the Year Awards ceremony, Times Mirror Building, Los Angeles, March 10, 1975. Quoted by permission. Title supplied by author.

[4] For biographical note, see Appendix.

Against Women in 1967, established a goal and an ideal that have gathered force. This year, 1975, is proclaimed by the United Nations as International Women's Year. Throughout the world a conscious effort is under way to bring women into a full participating role in social, economic and political leadership.

The acceptance of women in new fields is a recent phenomenon. Today the media acknowledges women as the "big story," and politics is no exception.

For example, when the national TV networks aired their usual election night extravaganzas last November, for the first time NBC and CBS had special commentators assigned to report exclusively throughout the evening on the way women were faring at the polls. Leslie Stahl reported for CBS and Barbara Walters for NBC.

The Los Angeles *Times,* however, was a bit ahead of NBC, CBS, and others. In 1950 Dorothy Chandler recognized the importance and significance of the contributions of women; and she initiated the Women of the Year Awards. Today's ceremony marks a quarter-century of this recognition.

There are difficult and taxing problems facing us at this moment. The industrial advances of the world community are rapidly devouring the supply of natural resources. Items that we have long taken for granted, have suddenly become critically scarce.

But in the first confusion of awakening to an unsure future of limitation and scarcity, we have overlooked a plentiful resource: human talent.

It is a tragic irony that we despair over deprivations about to be suffered, while seven and one half million able and creative Americans sit idle, their collective energy languishing.

We must come to realize that we are in another difficult period in our history when economic realignments and institutional changes must be undertaken.

With ingenuity and toil, coupled with the American

spirit, we will draw upon the abundant energy in our populace to advance the well-being of all our citizens.

And women will be called upon as never before. As a group they possess the largest reservoir of unused capacity, for they have been unemployed and underemployed more than the rest.

This is *not* because women have less education or aptitude. In fact, the record shows just the opposite. Women eighteen years of age and over in the labor force have slightly more schooling than the general population.

This is a paradoxical time. Women offer the most because society has advanced them the least.

At times of great stress societies have frequently set aside their previous prejudices and looked for leadership in uncommon places; Golda Meir and Indira Gandhi both were called to lead their countries in hours of crisis; and Franklin Roosevelt chose Frances Perkins in 1933 to be the first woman Cabinet member: Secretary of Labor—the focal point of New Deal reform.

Last week Carla Anderson Hills became Secretary of Housing and Urban Development, the third woman Cabinet member. . . . In the coming days more women will be called upon to lead.

In state legislatures across the country women made modest gains in 1974, increasing their representation from 5 to 8 percent. Several states deserve special mention: in New Hampshire there are 104 women legislators out of 424. In Arizona there are 18 women out of 90, and in Colorado 16 out of 100.

Women also made gains in 1974 in getting elected to statewide offices. Connecticut now has a woman governor, New York has a woman lieutenant governor and California and Minnesota have women secretaries of state. All told, 45 women hold statewide offices out of a total of 582.

I think we are starting to make significant progress. Consider this encouraging sign: in 1965 the Gallup Poll found the women most admired by Americans to be Mrs. John F.

Kennedy, Mrs. Lyndon B. Johnson, Queen Elizabeth, and
Mrs. Dwight D. Eisenhower. Three of the four obviously
won their place on the list by virtue of their marriages to
famous men. The fourth was there by birthright.

But nine years later the 1974 Gallup Poll reveals a much
different type of woman that Americans admire the most:
Golda Meir, Rose Kennedy, Shirley Chisholm, Indira
Gandhi, and Pat Nixon. These women earned the admira-
tion of Americans because of their own accomplishments.
(Some may claim that Pat Nixon is an exception, but since
she won this *Times* award in 1953 I don't think the subject
is open to debate.)

The Gallup Poll also made an interesting finding on a
national survey in 1970: 84 percent of the electorate said
they would vote for a qualified woman for Congress.

In the United States Congress today, 18 congresswomen
hold elected places beside 417 male Representatives. All represent varying viewpoints and all are quite different, from
Barbara Jordan to Bella Abzug—or from Pat Schroeder, a
thirty-two-year-old lawyer, to Millicent Fenwick, a former
Vogue editor and author of the *Vogue Book of Etiquette*
who at sixty-four is a freshman member.

And more will be coming to Congress as women win
their way into local and state offices, become visible as effective public leaders, and move into federal elected ranks.

At this unique point in history the aspirations of women
are in march step with the needs of the nation. We offer new
leadership in an uninspired time, a new supply of energy in
the void of scarcity, and the power of our collective spirit in
a time of apathy.

The aspirations of women will not go unrequited! They
are best expressed in a popular song by Frances Dana Gage,
sung at women's suffrage meetings one hundred years ago.
The song is called "One Hundred Years Hence," and it
appropriately expresses the aspirations of women for the
1970s:

One hundred years hence, what a change will be made,
In politics, morals, religion and trade,
In statesmen who wrangle or ride on the fence,
These things will be altered a hundred years hence.

Then woman, man's partner, man's equal shall stand
While beauty and harmony govern the land.
To think for oneself will be no offense,
The world will be thinking a hundred years hence.

Instead of speech making to satisfy wrong,
All will join the glad chorus to sing freedom's song
And if the millennium is not a pretense
We'll all be good brothers a hundred years hence.

A SHIFT IN THE BALANCE [5]

Virginia Y. Trotter [6]

The United Nations has declared 1975 International Women's Year. When President Ford signed an executive order launching US participation in the program, Mrs. Ford is reported to have said: "Congratulations, Mr. President. I'm glad to see that you have come a long, long way" (*Christian Science Monitor,* January 14, 1975). In recent months many have joined the President in traveling "the long way." In the 1974 fall elections 1,300 women competed for national and state offices. Connecticut elected Ella T. Grasso governor, and 18 women (16 Democrats and 2 Republicans) now serve in the House of Representatives (an increase of 2 over the previous session). Thirty-four states have ratified the Equal Rights Amendment (ERA), leaving approval by only four more states needed before the amendment becomes law. In each remaining state proponents of ERA are putting up hard-fought battles.

Conferences like the Academic Woman Conference at Kansas State University, February 15, 1975, are much in order. The speaker on this occasion was Virginia Y. Trotter, assistant secretary for education for the Department of Health, Education, and Welfare. Speaking to a predominantly female audience, Dr. Trotter, former dean at the University of Nebraska, recounted the gains made by women and counseled them on what they need to do if American women are to reach their highest potential.

More moderate in tone than some other activists in the women's movement, Dr. Trotter presents a well-prepared and carefully conceived speech. She assures her listeners, "It's only the beginning."

I'm delighted to be here with you today. As you know, all of my working life has been in the field of educaton, and this occasion gives me the unique opportunity to share some of my concerns on the future of women in leadership and decision-making positions in education.

It was almost two hundred years ago that Abigail Adams

[5] Delivered at the Academic Woman Conference, Kansas State University, Manhattan, February 15, 1975. Quoted by Permission.
[6] For biographical note, see Appendix.

wrote to her husband John at the Constitutional Convention:

Dear John:
By the way, in the new code of law I desire you would remember the ladies and be more generous and favorable to them, than were your ancestors. Remember, all men would be tyrants if they could.

Your loving wife, Abigail

He answered:
Depend on it my dear wife. We men know better than to repeal our masculine system.

When you think of it, America was already 144 years old before women received the right to vote. Fifty years ago our institutions were totally male dominated. And what is the situation today—50 years later? Out of a female population of about 107 million, there are not today 100 women in posts of command or in high supervisory or policy-making positions. Only 3 women have been elected to the Senate and 78 women have been chosen as Representatives to the House. There have been only 3 women governors, 2 women Cabinet members, and 14 women ministers and ambassadors.

Today, there are no women in the Cabinet, no women in the Senate, one woman governor, and only 18 women Representatives. The picture is the same in finance, business, and the media.

Almost all of the mass circulation women's magazines were once edited by women. Today most are edited by men.

Yesterday, most of the presidents of women's universities were women. Today, many have been replaced by men. One statistic alone suffices to reveal the situation in the world of education. In 1972, women comprised 57.6 percent of the professional educators in New York City public schools but only 1.7 percent of the high school principals were women. The University Council for Educational Administration determined in 1972 that only 2 percent of all professors of educational administration were women—and although women make up about 40 percent of the work force, only about 10 percent of them are managers at most. Perhaps nothing epitomizes the need for sensitivity and consciousness raising among educators more—than at a recent convention of school administrators in which there were two panel discussions relating to women:

(1) From Adam's Rib to Women's Lib—You've Come A Long Way Baby

(2) The Superintendent's Wife—Some Do's and Don'ts and Maybe's

It's true that a resolution was passed to identify women who are potential leaders, but nevertheless these titles say a lot about attitudes.

The truth of it is we have continued to maintain relatively undisturbed all the ancient edicts about the superiority of males and the inferiority of females. In short—what we call today the Women's Liberation Movement is only the most recent aspect of the struggle that began with Mary Wollstonecraft's *Vindication of the Rights of Women* in 1795.

I received just before I left for Kansas a report from the National Center for Education Statistics which will be sent to the President showing that the salaries of women relative to men have not significantly improved either in private or public institutions of higher education. Women's salaries were 82.9 percent of men's salaries in 1972, and they were 83.2 percent in 1974. Women were also disadvantaged in the tenure situation where 26.7 percent of the women and 57 percent of the men had tenure. In academic rank, for example, in 1972, the total number of full women professors was 9.8 percent and in 1974, 10.3 percent; women associate professors in 1972 numbered 16.3 percent and in 1974, 27.1 percent. The complete survey will be published at a later date, and I'd be very happy to send it to you.

Considering this gloomy picture, you may well ask what there is to look forward to in the future. But there is much to look forward to. Since 1970 there has been a *legislative explosion*—as Congress has recognized the necessity to end sex discrimination on the campus. Title IX now prohibits discrimination on the basis of sex in all federally assisted education programs, and after over ten thousand responses, the regulations are finally being prepared for release.

I believe the second great breakthrough favoring the goal of sex equality is the opening of the doors of higher education to women. Today, a girl can be admitted to college and get the same education as a boy, and she is free to study for any career that she aspires to. At least society now has access to women's brains and talents instead of only men's—but it is still woefully underutilized. As I have traveled from state to state, I see the development of new research centers and resource centers on women's studies. I see women faculty and students coming together to examine their status on the campus. I see an interchange and communication between diverse people, older and younger women, government and volunteer organizations, industry taking the initiative in new management training courses for women, Carnegie and Ford Foundation funding research projects on career aspirations. There are new innovative programs in recruitment and training procedures. Our own Fund for the Improvement of Postsecondary Education has initiated a most creative approach for career counseling for women, establishment of a woman's center for career and life planning, and a unique grant for research on reducing the attrition of women students in the sciences—to mention just a few.

However, the efforts to change education and employment patterns for women are part of a larger social concern. What we need to know is information about women who have aspired but failed, the conditions under which more women are likely to aspire, the specific job descriptions which detract from its desirability for women and what are the professional aspirations of women entering the universities. In fact, career aspiration has been identified as the crucial issue in women's education.

One of the greatest challenges is to convince women

themselves that they can go beyond the role stereotype that was formed in them virtually since birth. Little boys are given toys that challenge the mind and teach manual dexterity. Their sisters are given dolls and teacups and dreams of motherhood.

It has been said that girls become less intelligent as they grow older, that thousands of females who are positively brilliant in grade school become merely bright in high school, simply very good in college, and finally, almost mediocre in graduate school. But I doubt that any of us here accept that.

I believe as a result of the women's movement, more and more young women are rethinking their goals and aspirations and are planning lives that include active careers.

I believe women not only have the capacity to accept leadership but need to question themselves on what do women need to learn from men and what do men need to learn from women. Women in the working world must accept the responsibility of being assertive and to accept the reality of the demands of the job.

As women we must realize three fundamentals:

(1) A woman must be competent in whatever she decides to do because opportunity means nothing if we're not prepared to take advantage of it.

(2) Women as well as men must be aware of their prejudices against women in responsible positions. We absolutely cannot afford to maintain artificial barriers of race–sex–or creed—artificial barriers that prevent full use of all human resources.

(3) Women must become convinced within themselves that they can do what they most want to do—and they must expect to be looked upon as persons and be willing to accept the same responsibilities within a job that men are expected to accept.

This means living with the same professional strains and stresses that men live with—there is a difference—we have to be better, because most of us don't have "a wife" at home.

If we play our role as liberated women to the fullest—the future is going to hold a more honest and happier relationship between women and men—and between men and women and their country.

The seesaw—or the escalator—is an excellent image in that as the new gains and setbacks take effect, the sexes will only hamper progress if they see themselves at opposite ends of a seesaw, one falling as the other rises. It is by recognizing our mutual stakes in abandoning stereotypes that we can turn the seesaw into an escalator for lifting everybody as it goes along. It was stated eloquently by Dr. Matina Horner, president of Radcliffe College, who went to the heart of what is necessary, no matter what the ups and downs of governmental decree—when she said:

> There is an increasing awareness that the genuine experiences of equality between men and women depend not only on the opportunities and barriers society has to offer—but also and perhaps more importantly—on the reaction and beliefs that those men and women involved have about themselves and each other. Since people differ from each other as individuals—more than men and women do as groups—those who choose to pursue traditional careers or family patterns should be encouraged to do so with pride—without guilt, discomfort, or apology—just as those who seek nontraditional fulfillment and life patterns must also enjoy and exercise their options freely—without fear of retribution and loss of self-esteem.

But even if all job discrimination were to end tomorrow —nothing very drastic would change. For job discrimination is only part of the problem. It does impede women who choose to go higher up in industry, academia or government—but it does not by itself—help us to understand why so many women *choose* to be aides instead of physicians—assistants instead of executives—instructors instead of deans.

Discrimination frustrates choices already made—and something more pernicious perverts the motivation to choose. *That something* is an unconscious ideology about the nature of the female, an ideology which constricts the emerging self-image of a female child and the nature of her aspirations from the very first.

So long as those responsible for the education of children believe sexual stereotypes to be innate rather than culturally induced, so long will the conditioning continue.

We now know that children's aspirations are developed at a very early age—through the visual stimuli of mass communication. Through their interaction with role models, and through direct and indirect verbal messages children learn who is smart, who is powerful, who can be creative, who can be independent, who will be successful, and who will fail.

In school the expectation of "feminine" behavior is steadily reinforced by adult attitudes, curriculum materials, and various kinds of separate activities for boys and girls. But, lest you think that stereotyping is limited to men, let me assure you this is not the case. A study was made recently showing that women are equally guilty of self-defeating prejudice.

An equal number of professional monographs by male and female authors were selected. The articles covered a variety of subjects, and all were adjudged in advance to be of equal merit. But in order to test the reaction of college women who took part in the study, changes were made in the authors' names. Half of the articles written by a man were labeled with the name of a woman. Half of those written were labeled with a man's name. All of the articles purportedly written by men received a higher rating than those labeled as having a woman author. The results confirmed that these college women attribute a higher level of competence to the professional work of men than to that of their female counterparts.

Last Friday at a meeting with publishers of college books, a similar story was told of a young woman who chose to publish her book under her initials rather than her first name. She felt it would be more saleable. Maybe so—but this is a great area of weakness. If we can't comprehend the fact that we're all in this together—then it can never work. We are all part of a movement interested in obtaining equality and equity for all *human beings* and that is what is important. And that is why I believe that it is up to *you*— because it is the colleges and universities which are the key to any effort on the part of women to awaken more people to the whole matter of discrimination and understand why society perpetuates it.

I agree with John Stuart Mill when he said, "The knowledge men can acquire of women even as they have been and are without reference to what they might be is wretchedly imperfect and superficial and will always be so until women themselves have told us all they have to tell." But to consult only women when writing about women would be, I believe, to invite some of the same disabilities that would afflict a dominantly male approach to the subject.

It was of great interest to read about the Michael Korda book, *Male Chauvinism and How It Works.* He is a successful business executive who replays the games one by one that men play to keep women at the bottom of the organizational ladder. Some of you here today, I'm sure, are familiar how the table of organization can be changed to undercut a successful woman and what attitudes, language, and demands some men employ to hold women down. But what is *encouraging* is the *realization* that when men realize that they are seeing other people as stereotypes—whether from fear or habit—they make stereotypes of themselves.

Certainly the employment of increased numbers of women faculty members and administrators at high levels would have a considerable impact upon lessening discriminatory practices. Such a policy would give men and women students role-models of successful and respected academic women.

No one woman speaks for women, but I must say it is a great time to be a woman and to be part of one of the great challenges of our time. As teachers and administrators we have an unparalleled opportunity to effect change. Your roles on the transmission of values and on the preparation of men and women for careers make this opportunity a responsibility. Legislation can support equality but without the involvement of men and women together to give the law life and momentum, meaning and action, then nothing we can do in Washington can make a real difference.

The task of teaching, reorientation and facilitation are the primary tasks for women and will remain so until the goals we seek have become interwoven into the fabric of social consciousness.

How do we begin? First, by listening to ourselves, listening to our experiences, by listening deeply and humbly—but with a sense of trust and confidence that we can understand what our experience shows we require, for that is what the new image must incorporate. The old model of a "good woman" has become insufficient for life today. The old image has grown so small and narrow, and if women are not prepared to believe and to understand their own lives better than do men, they will not have the courage and stamina to change them.

What we have at this moment is the statement of history that it is necessary, that social change demands it. I believe it is important to realize how vital a new image of women is for humanity as a whole. A new image of women as active participants and leaders in society does not mean women will desert the emotional validity of personal relations as we move into the world of action. We will bring it along with us to a place where it is badly needed. What we need is the gift of a new image—one that shows men and women honestly and realistically, interrelating and active in all phases of life.

I am reminded of what Elizabeth Cady Stanton, at age seventy-two, said in speaking to the International Council of Women, in the year 1888:

The younger women are starting with great advantages over us. They have the results of our experience; they have superior opportunities for education; they will find a more enlightened public sentiment for discussion; they will have more courage to take the rights which belong to them. . . . Thus far women have been the mere echoes of men. Our laws and constitutions, our creeds and codes, and the customs of social life are all of masculine origin. The true woman is as yet a dream of the future.

I know and you know that the dream is possible because here we are today sharing these thoughts, caring about each other as men—as women—and caring how we effectively utilize together the greatest source of energy that our country possesses—ourselves!

I'm proud the federal government has provided the leadership and the opportunity for America's women to reach their highest potential—and it's only the beginning.

In two years our country will be celebrating its two hundredth birthday. Today, just as two hundred years ago, we are at a crucial turning point in our history. It is a time in which we must reaffirm our faith and commitment to the ideas and values upon which the United States of America was founded—not as an end in itself but as a means to rekindle the American tradition of individual initiative, restore pride in what we do and how we do it. Never has there been a more propitious time for change than the present. All the rest of history has been different in the sense that man and woman together have never had the power to take total destiny in their laps.

The grand leaps of the creative intelligence and resolute determination that pushed back the American frontier can now be put to work on the most magnificent project of all—men and women working together to create a world congenial not just to human physical presence but also to the human spirit.

PEOPLE POWER [7]

JOHN W. GARDNER [8]

John W. Gardner, who has been referred to as "Socrates in a navy blue suit," has put into motion since 1970 a most effective open citizens' lobby called Common Cause—with 300,000 members and an annual budget of $15 million. He is the hero of the consumer and a scourge to the politician, writes Louise Sweeney (*Christian Science Monitor,* February 20, 1974). Gardner has explained his number one priority on a list of critical issues in these words:

> Whether we have the kind of society in which individuals can participate, feel that they have some importance as individuals and aren't just anonymous numbers, grains of sand in a bucket, and this has to do with whether we have open, accessible, accountable government, responsive government. Because this is the citizen's most important instrument for getting a grip on this enormous, intricately organized society. . . . We want citizens who have an alive sense of being part of the community, part of the social venture.

Mr. Gardner was an excellent choice to address the spring meeting of the Public Affairs Research Council, Inc. (PAR), on April 3, 1975, at the Grand Ballroom of the Fairmont Hotel, New Orleans. The audience of four hundred was composed of members of PAR and Common Cause, as well as state and local officials, teachers, librarians, and other interested citizens.

Within the state of Louisiana PAR serves a function similar to that of Common Cause on the national scene. It is primarily a fact-finding organization, supported by private donations, that attempts to provide voters with insights into state problems and into activities and attitudes of state officials.

In his talk Gardner attempted to achieve two purposes: to promote the citizen's determination to gain responsiveness from elected officials and to promote good will toward both his own organization and PAR. His language is simple and concrete; his sentences, short and direct, and his supporting material, specific and pertinent. He impressed his listeners.

[7] Delivered to the spring meeting of the Public Affairs Research Council, Inc., Fairmont Hotel, New Orleans, April 3, 1975. Quoted by permission.

[8] For biographical note, see Appendix.

Gardner is described by Louise Sweeney as having "a calm and strong presence. . . . When he talks the voice is deep and meditative, with thoughtful pauses as though he's writing, rather than speaking. Clarity is important to this man with a powerful, distilled style, who wrote ten drafts of his last book."

The confidence of citizens in their instruments of self-government has reached a low point. And I must remind you that the drop in confidence didn't begin with Watergate. As long ago as 1960, John Kennedy was startled to discover that only 65 percent of the eligible electorate actually voted in the election that made him President. Twelve years later, in 1972, only 55 percent voted. We expect a lower turnout in off-year elections, but one has to be alarmed by the precipitous drop that occurred last November—a 39 percent turnout nationwide on election day. How much lower will we allow it to drop before we act to repair the mistrust?

There is only one way to repair the citizen's loss of confidence in our political and governmental institutions, and that is to make the institutions worthy of his confidence. We must build a political and governmental process that is open, accountable and unbought. This is the problem that underlies all the other problems. Until we tackle it, we will not solve the others. Corruption, backroom fixes, secret deals—quite aside from their moral repulsiveness—finally create government that just doesn't work. Finally, the "insiders" can't even save themselves. The intricately rigged system fails to serve even those who rigged it.

There are serious observers who believe that the ever-increasing complexity of our problems, has carried our society—and the world—beyond the reach of human manageability. I'm not prepared to accept that assertion. But if you think about it, and then observe this incredibly complex nation operating within a system that is often almost crippled by surreptitious pressures and arrangements, it's bound to send a chill up your spine.

And the chill up your spine will not diminish as you

observe the manner in which the nation has dealt with two great and imminent dangers that it faces today: the energy crisis and the economy. The possibility of a major depression is so real that people hesitate to speak of it. The likelihood that we could be drawn into war in the Mideast grows ever greater. People are freely predicting that within a year we will be in a depression or at war.

In the face of those grim realities, we observe an appalling vacuum of leadership in this country today. If you're a rabid Democrat you blame that on the White House. If you're a rabid Republican you blame it on the Congress. If you are neither you may blame both for the failure to act. If you're a historian you may be led to recall the letter which the elder Henry Cabot Lodge sent to Teddy Roosevelt during the coal strike of 1902, in which he said, "Isn't there something we could appear to be doing."

But finally you have to face the fact that the paralysis of leadership is due in part to the unseen grip of the special interests. When you think of a top policy maker trying to solve one or another of these problems, you might think of a man trying to win a game of checkers. Someone leans over his shoulder and puts a thumb on one checker, saying, "Go right ahead and play. Just don't move this checker." Someone else leans over the other shoulder and does the same with another checker. A third person walks up and immobilizes another checker. And so on. Pretty soon all thumbs, no moves.

Think of the thumbs as the special interests that come to play in almost every major government decision. The only unrealistic thing about the comparison is that in real life the thumbs are invisible. The owners of the thumbs don't really want to paralyze the whole process. Each just wants to immobilize one checker. But collectively, they prevent a solution.

Is that really a sensible way to run a complex nation in a dangerous world? You know it isn't. And I know it isn't. That's one of the reasons PAR exists. That's one of the reasons Common Cause exists. And between us, we're going to do something about it!

When the political process becomes the plaything of the special interests operating invisibly, the consequences fall upon virtually all citizens, consumers, taxpayers. Great problems go unsolved and no one can say why. Money leaks out of the pockets of the taxpayers, and they don't know where it goes. They elect people on promises and can't hold them to account. And they are the ones—citizens, consumers, taxpayers—who ultimately foot the bill for graft and corruption.

Most of you are familiar with what one nonpartisan citizens' movement, Common Cause, is trying to do about all of this. And the story of our brief life in pursuit of that goal is fairly spectacular.

When we announced, in the late summer of 1970, that we were founding a citizens' movement, veteran observers of the Washington scene greeted us with something between pity and derision. And no one can be quite so derisive as veteran Washington observers. They know all the reasons why something new can't possibly be done.

But the skepticism has vanished. The organization that was supposed to die in its cradle has in the past four years fought literally hundreds of tough battles in the Congress, the courts and the state legislatures, and we have won most of them. That's a matter of record.

At a time that is widely described as a time of citizen apathy, we grew in four years from zero to over 300,000 members, which for a citizens' organization is a very large number. In fact, Common Cause is the largest citizens' public affairs organization in the nation's history.

This organization that was supposed to be totally unrealistic, alerted the nation to the need for campaign finance reform two years before Watergate.

We sued both major parties for violating the Federal Corrupt Practices Act, and the suit helped prod Congress to pass the Federal Election Campaign Act of 1971. You now hear little about that statute, but it was of historic importance. For the first time it required full disclosure of political contributions—an astonishing and effective step forward.

We sued the committee to reelect the President and forced disclosure of the secret contributions prior to April 7, 1972. As you know, it turned out that among those secret contributions were funds which financed some of the most scandalous episodes of Watergate.

Then this fall we won an extraordinary victory. Congress passed a law which provided for a mixed public-private system of financing of presidential campaigns and set up an independent enforcement mechanism. At the beginning of the Ninety-third Congress not one of Washington's heavyweight political pundits would have given you a nickel for the chance of passing such a statute. Now it's the law of the land.

In 1973, Common Cause played the key outside lobbying role in persuading the House of Representatives to reverse its long tradition of secrecy and open up most of its bill-drafting sessions. And we played a key role in altering the archaic and tyrannical seniority system in Congress. In fact, we helped spark the greatest burst of congressional reform since 1946, more likely since 1910.

We set out to accomplish reform at the state level in four areas having to do with open and accountable government—campaign financing reform, lobbying disclosure, conflict-of-interest disclosure and open government. In the past two and a half years 46 out of the 50 states have passed major reforms on one or another of those issues. That is a totally unprecedented wave of reform in the states. It has never happened before in our history.

Now I want to turn to another subject—Common Cause plans for the period immediately ahead.

First of all we shall seek public financing of congressional elections.

What Congress did this year was to legislate a double

standard. They cleaned up presidential elections, but decided they didn't really want to clean up congressional elections. We're going to help them correct that omission.

During the recent election campaign, Common Cause members all over the country, pursuing what we call "issue politics," set out to obtain commitments from all candidates to support public financing of congressional campaigns. Of the winning candidates 242 have committed themselves on the record to support public financing—an ample majority of the House of Representatives.

The data gathered by Common Cause shows that special interest money flowed more heavily than ever in the 1974 congressional races—much more heavily. So there's still a grain of truth in the old saying that Congress operates by the golden rule, "He who has the gold makes the rules."

It is important to see what this means in terms of problems immediately before us such as unemployment, the recession, the energy shortage. To cope with such problems, Congress is going to have to do some tough things. Considering the source of campaign funds, one can see the difficulty Congress faces in doing any tough thing that offends the special interests. Remember the checkerboard.

The energy with which Common Cause members throughout the country sought commitments from candidates on reform measures yielded other important results. For example, 318 members—that's about three fourths of the new House of Representatives are committed to vote for a new lobbying disclosure law to replace the present Mickey Mouse statute. That is a spectacular result on an issue which the Ninety-third Congress didn't consider sufficiently important to devote as much as one minute of hearings to.

Similarly we have commitments from 266 members of the House to support a law for requiring personal financial disclosure by both legislative and executive branch offices.

We are going to tackle the executive branch to see if we can accomplish the same movement toward openness and accountability that we have helped to bring about in Congress and many state legislatures.

Now let me comment more generally on our approach to these problems.

Common Cause did not choose at random from the thousands of tasks we might have tackled to correct governmental deficiencies. We have clear, explicit and limited concerns with respect to government. We believe it should be accessible, accountable and responsive. The key word is accountability. The problem is not power as such—in the presidency, in the private sector or anywhere else. The problem is power that is not held accountable. And we have discovered that the most serious obstacles to that kind of government are *money* and *secrecy:* the scandalous capacity of money to buy political outcomes, and the old, bad political habit of doing the public's business behind closed doors. Those are the things you and we have to change.

A journalist recently described Common Cause as the most original political invention of modern times. I don't know whether he is right, but I do know that Common Cause is inserting new ingredients into the American political system. We are showing people new ways in which citizen action can be organized, financed and made effective. We are teaching citizens new ways of linking professional lobbying, litigation, grass-roots action, use of the media and "issue politics" on the campaign trail. We are demonstrating that in pursuing political goals, citizens need not be intimidated by the vastness and complexity of our society. We're proving that citizens can win.

High-minded citizens who look down on politics are going to have to learn that we need our politicians. Just as we must reject those who corrupt the public process, so must we support those politicians who risk their careers in the public interest. In any society, it is inevitable that equally worthy groups will want mutually incompatible things. Unless we want such differences settled by the whims of a dictator, or unless we want to shoot it out, we must turn to the much maligned arena of politics. We don't want to take the politics out of politics. We just want to take the rascals out of politics. We know we'll never wholly succeed. But we're going to make it a lot tougher for politicians to pursue rascality as a reputable way of life. We agree with the Chinese proverb that says, "You can't keep the birds of sorrow from flying over your head, but you keep them from building nests in your hair."

Modern trends in social organization make it urgently necessary to correct the powerlessness of the citizen. The whole trend of modern societies, whatever their ideology, is toward huge and complex organizational structures in which individual citizens feel ever more anonymous and helpless.

The urge to abuse power has not increased. But the means of exercising power have been dangerously strengthened. The enormous increases in the size of social groupings, the advances in communications technology and the development of new techniques of social control increase greatly the possibility of manipulating, deceiving or coercing the individual.

This may be the last chance citizens have to figure out ways of asserting themselves in relation to the huge and complex structures.

If we can show individuals how to throw a lasso of citizen accountability over the highest pinnacles of organized power, we may save our children from total subjugation by the interlocking processes of a technological society.

We are fighting the fight of everyone who believes that the individual—and individual responsibility—count for something. *We are asserting that individuals can have their say, even in the complex processes of modern society.* We are showing how it can be done.

Citizen action is not only good for the political system, it is very good for the citizens doing the acting. It gives them a feeling that citizens haven't had for a long, long time—that America is their venture, theirs to preserve, or theirs to neglect, and through neglect, perhaps to destroy.

The vitality and coherence of a society begins and ends with motivated people and the ideas they have in their heads of what their society is and ought to be. That's where it begins—and if it ends, that's where it ends.

Every summer millions of American citizens come to Washington—and bring their children—to visit our national shrines—the White House, the Capitol, the Washington, Jefferson and Lincoln monuments. But the spirit of the nation is not in the physical structures. It is in the hearts and minds of the citizens who come to look at the structures. If they stop believing, if they lose faith, if they stop caring, the monuments will be meaningless piles of stone, and the nation will be deader than the stones.

There will still be the land and the physical plant, and a lot of people milling around, but the historic venture that began with the Declaration of Independence—the venture we refer to familiarly as America—will be over. Dead. Finished.

In my judgment, that need not happen. In my judgment, if citizens stand up on their hind legs and act like free men and women, it will not happen.

Now let me close on a note of hope. Remember that word—*hope?* It used to be one of the main ingredients in the American consciousness. But for quite a while now, a lot of Americans have been on a no-hope diet—and it isn't good for them.

For my part, I find hope—not just hope, *great* hope—in the citizens of this country. There is still something resilient, courageous and everlastingly dependable about the American people. I take great hope in the new zeal with which citizen groups such as PAR, such as Common Cause, are tackling the problems facing our nation. There has never been a time in our history when citizen groups were better organized, or more willing to face tough issues or more skillful in battle.

We tend to idealize earlier generations of Americans; but when I observe the citizens who are acting today, I think that they are in important respects stronger and more mature than any preceding generation. Americans once had a sublimely unreasoning confidence in themselves, confidence that a beneficent providence would look after them. Citizens who are active today see the world more maturely. They know it's a hard world. They know there isn't a solution to every problem. They know that no human society can ever be perfect, and they know that there will be no utopias, and that humans themselves will never be perfect. They have a new hard-bitten morale that can face up to all those harsh truths and still strive with every ounce of energy to prevail.

And that new hard-bitten morale can be the saving of this nation. So I say "Strength to the PAR, strength to Common Cause, strength to all the citizen groups who are determined to make our system work. Keep it up! Turn the platoons into regiments and the regiments into armies. You can restore this nation."

Then this generation can die proud; not ashamed that in our time the great venture failed, but proud that we had the wisdom and the guts to save our heritage.

In less than eight months we will begin our Bicentennial year. The way to celebrate it is to work for the ideas of the Founding Fathers. When they wrote the Declaration of Independence and the Constitution, they didn't hand us a completed task. They handed us a set of objectives; they handed us a beginning. And we have had to work to make real the ideals expressed in our founding documents. Let 1976 find us deep in the struggle to create—in the words of the Declaration of Independence—a government "deriving its just powers from the consent of the governed." The Founding Fathers would not be at all surprised to find us—two hundred years later—still working on that. They knew that nothing is ever finally safe. They might say if they were here for the Bicentennial, "Struggling to keep our society free and open and vital is a beautiful way of celebrating. Forget the firecrackers."

THE BICENTENNIAL

FACTS AND THE FOUNDING FATHERS [1]

Virginius Dabney [2]

> But history, long after the passions and polemics of the
> time have been quieted, requires that any barrier be
> probed, whatever the cost, when persons have been defamed
> or truth injured or questions not asked (Julian P. Boyd,
> *The Papers of Thomas Jefferson*, Volume XVIII, p 679).

Fawn M. Brodie places the above quotation on the flyleaf of
her recent biography, *Thomas Jefferson: An Intimate History*
(Norton, 1974). After rereading Jeffersonian sources and reading
between the lines, she has produced a Book-of-the-Month Club
selection and a best seller. But if she has achieved success and
popularity, she has also upset or disturbed many historians and
devotees of Jefferson.

In a recent novel, *Burr*, Gore Vidal makes unkind references
to Jefferson and George Washington. He characterizes Washington
as "slow-witted" and makes reference to his "cold, dull, serpent
glance"; his "bleak, dark-toothed smile"; and his "cold, serpent's
nature."

Duly aroused by these two books, Virginius Dabney, the distinguished historian and retired editor of the Richard *Times-
Dispatch,* used them as the subject of his address at the 1975
Charter Day Convocation, held in the Phi Beta Kappa Hall at
the College of William and Mary, Williamsburg, Virginia. The
audience was composed of about seven hundred faculty members,
students, friends of the college, and state officials. Each year this
event is a special one at this ancient and distinguished institution, the second oldest college in the country and sometimes called
the "alma mater of a nation." The 1975 convocation marked the
282d anniversary of the granting of the royal charter and, of
course, the two hundredth anniversary of the American Revolution.

[1] Delivered at Charter Day Convocation, College of William and Mary, Williamsburg, Virginia, February 8, 1975. Quoted by permission.
[2] For biographical note, see Appendix.

"These best-selling volumes, purporting to be based on sound scholarship," Dabney asserts, "tend strongly to degrade some of the very men whom we, in the Bicentennial, are seeking to honor." His ceremonial speech thus has an argumentative tone and turns into countercriticism and almost a speech of refutation. Making Fawn Brodie his primary target, Dabney brings high ethos to his argument, using authority as his chief supporting material. He introduces opinions of three distinguished biographers: Julian P. Boyd, Dumas Malone, and Merrill Peterson. In addition, he offers a statement by Douglass Adair, a "profound student of the Jeffersonian era and one-time editor of the *William and Mary Quarterly*." He presents evidence to disprove the charge that Jefferson was guilty of fathering five children by the slave Sally Hemings. He dismisses the views of Aaron Burr because of Burr's hatred of Jefferson and cites other historians' treatment of Washington. And he says, in summation, "After mature reflection, I have concluded that the opinions of Douglas Freeman, James Flexner, Dumas Malone and John Richard Green outweigh those of Gore Vidal."

The reviewers, although not unanimous, seem to agree with Dabney in his evaluation. Although they commend Brodie for her industry, they think that her inferences are fragile and that her psychological analysis of Jefferson's guilt feelings is questionable.

Dabney's speech was quoted widely, in *Time* magazine, the New York *Times* (February 17, 1975), in the Richmond *Times-Dispatch* (February 9, 1975), and in full in *Vital Speeches of the Day* (April 15, 1975). Throughout his life, Dabney has been a frequent speaker before college and Phi Beta Kappa groups.

It is fitting that at the ancient College of William and Mary, whose halls have been trod by so many of the great men in our early history, we should concern ourselves on this Charter Day with the two hundredth anniversary of the American Revolution and our country's founding.

The men and women who carried the Continental Army to victory after years of intense struggle against apparently overwhelming odds, and then created a nation, deserve our veneration. They were not perfect, they had their faults and frailties, but they possessed ability, courage, determination and character.

There was a musical show a few years ago entitled *1776*. It did not purport to portray history as it was. Thomas Jefferson as a mooning, dreamy, not altogether bright individual certainly seemed a travesty on the original, and Richard Henry Lee as a song-and-dance man was so far removed from reality that nobody, let us hope, took *1776* seriously as a picture of actual persons and events.

But two books have appeared recently, both choices of the Book-of-the-Month Club, that are in a quite different category. At the very time when we are preparing to exalt those who brought the United States of America into being, and to pay tribute to their virtues and their accomplishments, *Burr* by Gore Vidal and *Thomas Jefferson* by Fawn Brodie have been published. These best-selling volumes, purporting to be based on sound scholarship, tend strongly to degrade some of the very men whom we, in the Bicentennial, are seeking to honor.

The Brodie book is not objectionable simply because it advances wholly unproved charges against Thomas Jefferson. It is even more objectionable because it seeks to show that the alleged fathering of a brood of mulatto children affected Jefferson's whole life thereafter, giving him a guilt complex. One of numerous farfetched interpretations advanced by Mrs. Brodie is that "the unwritten and unadmitted tragedy of Jefferson's life" was that he had to "keep up an elaborate pretense" that his relations with Sally Hemings, the mother of the children, did not exist. Evidence of this so-called tragedy has somehow escaped Jefferson's other biographers.

It should be recognized at the outset that the charge of fathering mulatto children was first circulated against Jefferson by a vicious, unscrupulous drunkard named James T. Callender, who had become furious with President Jefferson because the President refused to appoint him postmaster at Richmond.

While proof of Callender's allegation is wholly lacking, there is no question that, when young and single, Jefferson tried to seduce the wife of his friend, John Walker, when Walker was absent on a trip. This was admitted by Jefferson, who was obviously no plaster saint, and his modern biographers do not try to make him out one. They are aware of his faults, and this is obvious in their books about him.

But the three greatest living authorities on Thomas Jefferson all agree that Mrs. Brodie's book is based on half-truths, unwarranted assumptions and grievous misinterpretation of the known facts.

All three of them—Dumas Malone, Julian P. Boyd and Merrill Peterson—have devoted the greater part of their adult years to the study of Jefferson, in contrast to Mrs. Brodie, whose other books have been in entirely unrelated fields. These superlative scholars have provided me with heretofore unpublished statements concerning the Brodie book, which they have authorized me to use at this time. Their views were completely shared by the late Douglass Adair, profound student of the Jeffersonian era and one-time editor of the *William and Mary Quarterly*.

Dumas Malone, whose magisterial biography of Jefferson is regarded by authorities on both sides of the Atlantic as the last word on the subject, was reluctant to comment on the Brodie volume, saying that as a rule he did not discuss "other people's books on Thomas Jefferson." His statement is too long for me to quote it in full, but I give the following extract:

This determined woman runs far beyond the evidence and carries psychological speculation to the point of absurdity. The resulting mishmash of fact and fiction, surmise and conjecture is not history as I understand the term. . . .

Mrs. Brodie is not without insight into Jefferson's personality, and except for her obsession, might have contributed to our understanding of him. But to me the man she describes in her more titillating passages is unrecognizable.

She presents virtually no evidence that was not already known to scholars, and wholly disregards testimony which I regard as more reliable. . . .

Fawn Brodie and Gore Vidal cannot rob Washington and Jefferson of their laurels, but they can scribble graffiti on their statues. It is unfortunate that dirty words are so hard to erase, and it is shocking that the scribblers should be so richly rewarded.

Julian P. Boyd, editor of the massive collection of Jefferson's papers, whose colossal scholarship is universally recognized, terms "the principal defect of Brodie's work the manipulation of evidence, the failure to give due weight to the overwhelming considerations of fact and plausibility which conflict with her preconceptions."

Dr. Boyd points out that "among the whole chorus of adulatory critics of Mrs. Brodie's book, not a single Jefferson scholar is to be found. Mrs. Brodie's Jefferson never existed. . . . He is as fictional as the Jefferson in Vidal's *Burr*," Boyd says. He repudiates completely Brodie's picture of a "despairing, ambivalent, indecisive, guilt-ridden man."

Testimony of two aged blacks, published in the Pike County, Ohio, *Republican* in 1873, on which Mrs. Brodie relies heavily, was "obviously prompted by someone for some unexplained purpose," says Boyd, "being unquestionably shaped and perhaps even written and embellished by the prompter." Malone terms it "in the tradition of political enmity and abolitionist propaganda."

One impressive fact, which Mrs. Brodie ignored, was that one of the aged men professed to have personal recollections of events that occurred before he was born.

Merrill Peterson, greatly respected Jeffersonian scholar and author of *The Jefferson Image in the American Mind* and *Thomas Jefferson and the New Nation*, says concerning the Brodie book:

Mrs. Brodie has her obsessive theory and she sends it tracking through the evidence, like a hound in pursuit of game . . . in the end nothing is cornered and we are as remote from the truth as when we began. . . . I see no need to charge off in defense of Jefferson's integrity when we have no solid grounds for doubting it.

Dr. Peterson adds that Callender's newspaper article of 1802,

without supporting evidence of any kind, is the principal source of the legend, and in all likelihood we would not be discussing it today, but for him.

The legend was born in the malignant political climate of 1800; it was revived by abolitionists, for whom it disclosed the ultimate corruption of slavery . . . and it enjoys some currency today because of intense curiosity about history of the black man in America. . . . Callender's known character, his motives, his talent for libel—none of this damages his credibility for Mrs. Brodie.

Douglass Adair has an entire chapter entitled "The Jefferson Scandals" in his recently published posthumous volume *Fame and the Founding Fathers*. In it he makes the following statement:

In four widely separated areas of the country, four different scholars independently discovered four key documents, no one of which alone solves the puzzle, but which, when checked and crosschecked against each other, together throw a great blaze of light on Jefferson as a slaveholder, on the Monticello slaves, and in particular on the slave named Hemings. Today it is possible to *prove* that Jefferson was innocent of Callender's charges.

Adair's chapter on Jefferson was written in 1960. His assertion that the four documents referred to "prove" Jefferson's innocence seems a bit strong. It is almost impossible at this late date to *prove* such a thing beyond the shadow of a doubt. But it is altogether possible to indicate, on the basis of these documents, that the master of Monticello was almost certainly innocent. All the probabilities point in that direction.

The four documents referred to by Adair are Jefferson's *Farm Book,* a letter from Henry S. Randall to James Parton, the statement of Madison Hemings published in Ohio in 1873 and reminiscences of Isaac Jefferson, another slave at Monticello.

Jeffersonian scholars have studied these materials for years and they have all concluded that Jefferson was innocent. They believe with Adair that Peter Carr, son of Dabney Carr and Jefferson's sister, Martha, was the father of the mulatto children in question. They believe further that Peter's brother Sam was the father of another group of mulattoes.

Thomas J. Randolph, Jefferson's grandson, told the historian Henry S. Randall, that Sally Hemings was the mistress of Peter and her sister Betsey, the mistress of Samuel—and from these relationships sprang the progeny which resembled Mr. Jefferson. The Hemings girls' "connection with the Carrs was perfectly notorious at Monticello, and scarcely disguised by the latter—never disavowed by them," said Randolph.

He further declared that he showed Peter and Sam a newspaper containing an insulting article about Jefferson's supposed paternity of the children. In Randolph's words:

"Peter read it, tears coursing down his cheeks, and then handed it to Samuel. Samuel also shed tears. Peter exclaimed: 'Aren't you and I a couple of . . . pretty fellows to bring this disgrace on our poor uncle who has always fed us! We ought to be . . . by . . . !'" (Expletives deleted.)

Ellen Randolph Coolidge, granddaughter of Jefferson, wrote that Peter Carr had been overheard to say, with a laugh, that "the old gentleman had to bear the blame of his and Sam's misdeeds."

As corroborative evidence we have the statement of Edmund Bacon, overseer at Monticello, who said he knew who the father of Sally's children was, and it was not Thomas Jefferson. He did not name the father, but said, "I have seen him come out of her [Sally's] room many a morning when I went up to Monticello very early."

Why did Thomas Jefferson never deny publicly that he fathered these children? The most plausible explanation is that his father-in-law, John Wayles, had undoubtedly sired Sally Hemings, Jefferson's supposed paramour, and five additional children by Betty Hemings. In other words, this group of six illegitimates at Monticello were Jefferson's wife's half-sisters and brothers. With his father-in-law producing one group of mulattoes and his nephews producing two similar broods, it is easy to see why Jefferson was unwilling to enter into public controversy concerning this matter.

Despite Mrs. Brodie's repeated assertions that Jefferson had Sally Hemings for his concubine over a period of many years, she reaches the remarkable conclusion that his "heroic image remains untarnished and his genius undiminished." Yet she asserts that the affair gave him a guilt complex for the rest of his life.

Mrs. Brodie even tosses off the charge that George Wythe, perhaps the most venerated man of the age, was the father of the mulatto boy who died from the same poisoned coffee that killed Wythe. She makes no attempt whatever to offer proof.

Mrs. Imogene E. Brown, who has recently completed a biography of Wythe after several years of work, and Julian Boyd, who wrote a forty-five-page monograph on *The Murder of George Wythe,* both say there is absolutely no foundation for this charge. Merrill Peterson and Dumas Malone term it sheer fantasy.

It is dismaying that Mrs. Brodie's confused and confusing book has been so highly praised by some non-Jeffersonian scholars in the universities. Written by a professor of history, it has been lauded by other professors of history. Just what this signifies for the deterioration of standards on the faculties of our seats of learning I leave to others to determine.

The other book that we are considering today was not written by a professor of history, but by a novelist who makes pretensions to historical knowledge. *Burr,* by Gore Vidal, is even more objectionable than *Jefferson* by Brodie, since it defames both Washington and Jefferson.

I have been astounded by the number of people who have taken this book seriously.

One reason perhaps is to be found in the declaration of the publisher on the jacket. "The facts are actual," we are told, "and the portraits of the major characters, Washington, Jefferson, Hamilton . . . are drawn from their own words and from the observations of their contemporaries." Also, "The book creates with scrupulous accuracy . . . the most significant years in the history of America." Vidal himself says that "the story told is history and not invention."

Let us first look at this so-called history as it concerns George Washington.

The story is related largely in the words, or supposed words, of Aaron Burr, not the most admirable character in American history, who, it should be noted, hated both Washington and Jefferson.

He hated Washington from the time when the latter caught him in 1776 reading confidential papers on his desk. Washington had returned suddenly after leaving the room. The commander in chief gave Major Burr a well-deserved tongue-lashing. Burr's first biographer, who knew him for forty years, wrote that "his prejudices against General Washington were immovable."

In Vidal's book, Burr is constantly sneering at Washington, without any explanation by the author of the reasons for this bitterness. Nothing is said concerning the fact that Washington caught him reading confidential documents. Burr repeatedly makes slurring observations concerning Washington's appearance, his character and his ability. Yet we are told that this is a portrait drawn from Washington's "own words and the observations of his contemporaries."

Of course, there were contemporaries in the opposition party, as was Burr, who denounced Washington on all kinds of ridiculous grounds, and who simply invented charges when this appealed to them. Anybody can go through the records and find these statements. For example, the Philadelphia *Aurora*, the country's leading Republican paper, said when the first President of the United States completed his second term and retired to private life, that the master of Mount Vernon was "the cause of all the misfortunes of our country . . . every heart ought to beat high with exultation that the name of Washington from this day ceases to give currency to political iniquity and to legalize corruption."

Those who today may have reservations concerning the American press will doubtless concede that anything as preposterous as the foregoing will hardly be found in any leading twentieth century American newspaper.

But this is the sort of thing that Vidal seems to have relied on for the observations of "Washington's contemporaries." And the contemporary who is relied on more than any, of course, is Aaron Burr.

Washington, says Burr, ultimately "might be judged as an excellent politician who had no gift for warfare . . . an incompetent general." He adds that "in my view, had [Horatio] Gates or [Charles] Lee been placed in command of the Army, the war would have ended at least three years sooner."

Washington, needless to say, made his mistakes, including some bad ones, in the War of the Revolution, and he could not have won without the aid of France. But let us consider the enormous handicaps under which he labored and the fact that his sometimes ragged and starving, and always poorly equipped, army was facing soldiers from what was then the most powerful nation on the globe.

With respect to the Father of His Country's personal characteristics, we are informed by Burr that he was "slow-witted" but "no man was cleverer when it came to business and the promotion of his own commercial interests." One bit of evidence not mentioned by Burr is that the greedy and grasping Washington served seven years as commander in chief of the Continental Army and eight years as President of the United States, and refused to accept compensation in either post. He even spent some of his own funds for expenses.

Reference is made to his "cold, dull, serpent's glance," his "bleak, dark-toothed smile" and his "cold, serpent's nature." Also, he never read "any book at all." All this is what Vidal terms "history, not invention."

The one and only time that Vidal, or Burr, can bring himself to praise Washington, even halfheartedly, is when he speaks of him as "the supreme creator of this Union," but adds that he achieved this by his "powerful will and serpentine cunning."

The existence of this reptilian George Washington seems to have eluded his principal biographers. He has been intensively studied by Douglas S. Freeman and James T. Flexner, who probably, at a conservative estimate, devoted ten times as many hours to this enterprise as Gore Vidal. Freeman's massive biography got the Pulitzer Prize and Flexner's the National Book Award and a special Pulitzer citation. After the most thorough study ever made by anybody of Washington, Freeman failed to make a single reference to serpent's glances or serpentine cunning, and termed him "greater than any of us believed he was." Flexner called him "the indispensable man." Dumas Malone, who is completing the definitive biography of Thomas Jefferson, nevertheless regards Washington as the greatest of all Americans. The English historian, John Richard Green, in his classic *Short History of the English People,* said of Washington: "No nobler figure ever stood in the forefront of a nation's life."

After mature reflection, I have concluded that the opinions of Douglas Freeman, James Flexner, Dumas Malone and John Richard Green outweigh those of Gore Vidal.

Among those who knew Washington best were the members of the Virginia General Assembly, a body in which he had served several terms before the revolution. In 1785 they commissioned the foremost sculptor in Europe, Houdon, to execute his statue from life, and place it in the capitol at Richmond, in recognition of his services to the nation. In 1788, before Washington became President, the people of Richmond began celebrating his birthday annually as a holiday. If the description of Washington in *Burr* is based on the observations of his contemporaries, as the book's jacket claims, why was no reference made to such contemporaries as these, who paid him such conspicuous honor? Or those who demanded unanimously that he become the first President of the United States?

Vidal's and Burr's strictures on Thomas Jefferson are not

quite so startling as those on George Washington, since Burr
could hardly have failed to feel strong hostility toward Jefferson, in view of the latter's role in Burr's trial for treason.
President Jefferson did his best to obtain a conviction, and
his methods toward that end, it must be conceded, do not
show him in his best light.

It is understandable, then, that in the book Burr terms
his implacable enemy "a hypocrite" and "the most deceit-
ful" man he had ever known. Burr also repeats the old
canard that "wise Tom preferred the safety of Virginia and
the excitement of local politics to the dangers of war."

But when he refers to perhaps the most brilliantly versa-
tile man America has produced as "an intellectual dabbler"
who "never did any one thing particularly well," he lapses
into absurdity. He becomes still more nonsensical by
strongly implying that Jefferson couldn't even write, for he
says that certain words of the master of Monticello display
"a more than usual infelicity of style."

Burr even sneers at John Marshall, the man who saved
him from conviction on charges of treason. He states that in
the crucial opinion that secured his acquittal, Marshall
moved "with elephantine grace away from his own earlier
position," and Burr adds that the Chief Justice underwent
"a shameful collapse before Jefferson and public opinion."

Yet all this defaming of Washington, Jefferson and Marshall is hardly surprising, given Burr's tremendous prejudice
against Virginians. "Putting aside honor like a Virginian"
is one of his choice phrases. Only James Madison, among all
the Virginians, qualified as a gentleman, in Burr's opinion.
We inhabitants of the Old Dominion would be inclined to
regard this judgment as slightly excessive.

The amazing thing about Vidal's *Burr* and Brodie's *Jefferson* is that so many supposedly intelligent readers seem
to take them seriously. It is understandable that these books
have sold well, for almost any reasonably literate work that
makes sensational charges against revered figures or down-
grades those whom we have been taught to honor, will ap-

peal to the groundlings. It is, however, dismaying that persons of presumed discrimination have accepted the slanders in these volumes.

Here at the College of William and Mary, where so many of the foremost men in our early history studied, and in Williamsburg, where the heroic Virginians of the revolutionary era made some of the epochal decisions in our annals, it is peculiarly appropriate that we denounce these untruths and half-truths for what they are.

The shades of Washington, Jefferson, Marshall, Wythe, Patrick Henry, George Mason, Peyton Randolph, Richard Henry Lee and a host of others who made this nation, look down upon us here, as we celebrate Charter Day at this fine old institution of higher learning, and as we move into the Bicentennial. Let us remember their great and gallant services, and let us keep faith with them in gratitude for their lasting contributions to the founding of the Republic.

APPENDIX

BIOGRAPHICAL NOTES

BURKE, YVONNE BRATHWAITE (1932–). Born, Los Angeles, California; B.A., University of California at Los Angeles, 1953; J.D., University of Southern California, 1956; admitted, California bar, 1956; member, California State Assembly (Democrat), 1966–72; member, US House of Representatives, 1973– ; member, numerous boards and commissions.

BUTZ, EARL LAUER (1909–). Born, Albion, Indiana; B.S.A., with distinction, Purdue University, 1932; Ph.D., 1937; instructor, agricultural economics, Purdue University, 1937–39; assistant professor, 1939–43; associate professor, 1943–46; professor, head, Department of Agricultural Economics, 1946–54; dean, College of Agriculture, 1957–67; dean, College of Continuing Education and vice president, Research Foundation, 1968–71; assistant secretary, US Department of Agriculture, 1954–57; unsuccessful candidate for Republican nomination for governor of Indiana, 1968; secretary, US Department of Agriculture, 1971– ; director, numerous corporations; author, *The Production System for Farmers,* 1944; *Price Fixing for Food Stuffs,* 1952; articles in various pamphlets and farm bulletins. (See also *Current Biography: July 1972.*)

DABNEY, VIRGINIUS (1901–). Born, University (now Charlottesville), Virginia; A.B., University of Virginia, 1920; A.M., 1921; honorary degrees, University of Richmond, 1940; Lynchburg College, 1944; College of William and Mary, 1944; teacher, French and algebra, Episcopal High School, Alexandria, Virginia, 1921–22; reporter, Richmond *News Leader,* 1922–28; member, editorial staff, Richmond *Times-Dispatch,* 1928–34; chief editorial writer, 1934–36; editor, 1936–69; visiting lecturer, Princeton University, 1939–40; Cambridge University, 1954; Guggenheim fellow, 1968; recipient, Lee Editorial Award of Virginia Press Association and Washington and Lee University, 1937; Pulitzer Prize for editorial writing, 1947; National Editorial Award of Sigma Delta Chi, 1948, 1952; George Mason Award, 1969; Thomas Jefferson Award for public service, 1972; grant, National Endowment for the Humanities, 1970; member, board of directors, Richmond Public Library, 1943–61; member, American Society of Newspaper Editors; director, 1949–59; president, 1957–58; president Virginia Historical Society, 1969–72; member, Phi Beta Kappa, Delta Kappa Epsilon, Sigma Delta Chi (fellow), Society of Cincinnati, Jamestown Society; author, *Below the Potomac,* 1942; *Dry Messiah: The Life of Bishop Cannon,* 1949; *Virginia, the New Dominion,* 1971; contributor, leading magazines. (See also *Current Biography: September 1948.*)

DENNIS, DAVID WORTH (1912–   ). Born, Washington, D.C.; A.B., Earlham College, 1933; LL.B., Harvard Law School, 1936; admitted, Indiana bar, 1936; associate, Rupe, Brown & Reller, Richmond, Indiana, 1936–39; prosecuting attorney, Wayne County, Indiana, 1939–43; partner in own law firms, Richmond, Indiana, 1947–71; member, Indiana House of Representatives (Republican), 1947–49, 1953–59; member, US House of Representatives, 1969–75; US Army, lieutenant, junior grade, 1944–46.

EILBERG, JOSHUA (1921–   ). Born, Philadelphia, Pennsylvania; B.S., Wharton School, University of Pennsylvania, 1941; J.D., Temple University, 1948; admitted, Pennsylvania bar, 1948; private law practice, Philadelphia, 1948–52, 1954–   ; member, Eilberg, Carson & Getson, 1968–   ; assistant district attorney, Philadelphia, 1952–54; member, Pennsylvania General Assembly, 1954–66; member, US House of Representatives, (Democrat, Pennsylvania), 1967–   ; USNR, lieutenant, senior grade, 1942–46.

FLOWERS, WALTER (1933–   ). Born, Greenville, Alabama; A.B., University of Alabama, 1955; LL.B., 1957; Rotary Foundation fellow, University of London, 1957–58; admitted, Alabama bar, 1957; partner, Flowers and Shelby, 1961–68; member, US House of Representatives (Democrat, Alabama), 1968–   ; US Army, 1958–59; member, Phi Beta Kappa, Omicron Delta Kappa, Phi Delta Phi.

FORD, GERALD RUDOLPH (1913–   ). Born, Omaha, Nebraska; B.A., University of Michigan, 1935, LL.B., Yale Law School, 1941; admitted, Michigan bar, 1941; private law practice, Grand Rapids, Michigan, 1941–49; member, US House of Representatives (Republican, Michigan), 1949–73; minority leader, 1965–73; appointed Vice President by President Nixon, confirmed by Congress, December 6, 1973; became President upon resignation of Nixon, August 9, 1974; USN, 1942–46. (See also *Current Biography: March 1961.*)

FULBRIGHT, JAMES WILLIAM (1905–   ). Born, Sumner, Missouri; A.B., University of Arkansas, 1925; Rhodes scholar, B.A., Oxford University, 1928; M.A., 1931; LL.B., with distinction, George

Washington University, 1934; many honorary degrees; admitted, District of Columbia bar, 1934; special attorney, Antitrust Division, US Department of Justice, 1934–35; instructor, law, George Washington University, 1935–36; lecturer, law, University of Arkansas, 1936–39; president, University of Arkansas, 1939–41; member, US House of Representatives (Democrat, Arkansas), 1943–45; chairman, delegation to London Conference of Allied Ministers of Education, 1944; member, US Senate, 1945–75; chairman, Senate Foreign Relations Committee, 1959–75; instrumental in establishing program for American scholars to study abroad; member, Phi Beta Kappa; author, *Old Myths and New Realities, and Other Commentaries,* 1964. (See also *Current Biography: October 1955.*)

GARDNER, JOHN WILLIAM (1912–). Born, Los Angeles, California; A.B., Stanford University, 1935; A.M., 1936; Ph.D., University of California, 1938; many honorary degrees; teaching assistant, psychology, University of California, 1936–38; instructor, Connecticut College, 1938–40; assistant professor, Mt. Holyoke College, 1940–42; head, Latin American section, Federal Communications Commission, 1942–43; staff member, Carnegie Corporation, New York City, 1946–47; executive associate, 1947–49; vice president, 1949–55; president, 1955–65; consultant, 1968–70; president, Carnegie Foundation for the Advancement of Teaching, 1955–65; secretary, US Department of Health, Education, and Welfare, 1965–68; chairman, Urban Coalition, 1968–70; chairman, Common Cause, 1970– ; recipient, USAF Exceptional Services Award, 1956; Presidential Medal of Freedom, 1964; member, Woodrow Wilson Foundation, 1960–63; USMCR, 1943–46; author, *Excellence: Can We Be Equal and Excellent Too?* 1961; *Self-Renewal: The Individual and the Innovative Society,* 1964; *No Easy Victories,* 1968; *Recovery of Confidence,* 1970; *In Common Cause,* 1972; editor, *To Turn the Tide,* 1962. (See also *Current Biography: March 1956.*)

HATFIELD, MARK ODOM (1922–). Born, Dallas, Oregon; B.A., Willamette University, 1943; M.A., Stanford University, 1948; numerous honorary degrees; resident assistant, Stanford University, 1947–49; instructor, political science, Willamette University, 1949; dean of students, associate professor, 1950–56; member, Oregon House of Representatives, 1951–55; member, Oregon Senate, 1955–57; secretary of state, Oregon, 1957–59; governor, 1959–67; member, US Senate (Republican, Oregon), 1967– ; USNR, 1943–46. (See also *Current Biography: November 1959.*)

HUTCHINS, ROBERT MAYNARD (1899–). Born, Brooklyn, New York; A.B., Yale, 1921; LL.B., magna cum laude, 1925; honorary

A.M., Yale University, 1922; dean, Yale Law School, 1928–29; president, University of Chicago, 1929–44; chancellor, 1944–51; associate director, Ford Foundation, 1951–54; chief executive officer, Fund for the Republic, 1954– ; president, Center for the Study of Democratic Institutions, 1954–74; US Army, ambulance service, 1917–19; Croce di Guerra (Italy), 1918; member, Phi Beta Kappa, Order of the Coif, numerous honorary and learned societies; author, *The Higher Learning in America*, 1936; numerous other books and magazine articles. (See also *Current Biography: February 1974*.)

JAMES, DANIEL, JR. (1920–). Born, Pensacola, Florida; B.S., Tuskegee Institute, 1942; graduate, Air Command and Staff College, Maxwell Air Force Base, 1957; honorary degrees, University of West Florida, 1971; University of Akron, 1973; Virginia State College, 1974; instructor, Civilian Pilot Training Program, Tuskegee Institute, 1942–43; commissioned second lieutenant, USAF, 1943; served as flight leader, assistant commander, and commander with fighter squadrons in the Philippines, Korea, England, Libya, Thailand, United States; flew 101 combat missions, Korean war, 78 combat missions, Vietnam war; deputy assistant secretary of defense (public affairs), US Department of Defense, 1970–73; promoted to lieutenant general, 1973– ; vice commander, Military Airlift Command, Scott Air Force Base, Illinois, 1974– ; recipient, Department of Defense Distinguished Service Medal, Air Force Distinguished Service Medal, Legion of Merit with one oak leaf cluster, Distinguished Flying Cross with two oak leaf clusters, Meritorious Service Medal, Air Medal with thirteen oak leaf clusters, Distinguished Unit Citation Emblem with one oak leaf cluster, Presidential Unit Citation Emblem with one oak leaf cluster, Republic of Korea Presidential Unit Citation Ribbon.

JORDAN, BARBARA C. (1936–). Born, Houston, Texas; B.A., magna cum laude, Texas Southern University, 1956; J.D., LL.B., Boston University, 1959; admitted, Massachusetts and Texas bars, 1959; administrative assistant to county judge, Harris County, Texas; member, Texas Senate, 1967–72; member, US House of Representatives (Democrat, Texas), 1973– ; member, board of directors, National Urban League, 1970–72.

KISSINGER, HENRY ALFRED (1923–). Born, Fürth, Germany; B.A., summa cum laude, Harvard, 1950; M.A., 1952; Ph.D., 1954; arrived, United States, 1938; naturalized, 1943; executive director, Harvard International Seminar, 1951–60; lecturer, government, Harvard University, 1957–59; associate professor, 1959–62; professor, 1962–69; director, special studies project, Rockefeller Brothers Fund, Inc., 1956–59; consultant to Presidents Eisenhower, Kennedy, Johnson; assistant to President, for national security affairs, 1969– ; secretary, US Department of State, 1973– ; US Army, 1943–46; recipient Bronze Star; member, Phi Beta Kappa; author, *Nuclear Weapons and Foreign Policy*, 1957; *A World Restored*, 1957; *The Necessity For Choice: Prospects of American Foreign Policy*, 1961; *The Troubled Partnership: A Reappraisal of the Atlantic Alliance*, 1965; *American Foreign Policy: Three Essays*, 1969; over forty articles in various journals. (See also *Current Biography: June 1972*.)

McBATH, JAMES HARVEY (1922–). Born, Watertown, South Dakota; B.S., Northwestern University; M.A., 1947; Ph.D., 1948; assistant professor, speech, University of New Mexico, 1950–52; University of Iowa, 1953–54; assistant professor, European program, University of Maryland, 1954–56; associate professor, University of Southern California, 1957–63; professor, 1963– ; chairman, Department of Speech Communication, 1965– ; president, American Forensic Association, 1960–62; Western Speech Communication Association, 1968; Delta Sigma Rho-Tau Kappa Alpha, 1969–72; Association of Departments and Administrators in Speech Communication, 1975; sergeant, US Army Air Force, 1943–46; coauthor, *British Public Address*, 1971; *Guidebook for Speech Communication*, 1973; editor, *Argumentation and Debate*, 1963; journal, American Forensic Association, 1966–68; numerous articles in various magazines.

NIXON, RICHARD MILHOUS (1913–). Born, Yorba Linda, California; B.A., Whittier College, 1934; LL.B., Duke University, 1937; private law practice, Whittier, California, 1937–41; attorney, Office of Emergency Management, Washington, D.C., 1942; member, US House of Representatives (Republican, California), 1947–51; member, US Senate, 1951–53; Vice President of the United States, 1953–61; unsuccessful Republican candidate for President, 1960; resumed law practice, Los Angeles, 1961–63; New York City, 1963–68; President of the United States, 1969–74 (resigned August 9); lieutenant commander, USN, 1942–46; author, *Six Crises*, 1962. (See also *Current Biography: December 1969*.)

ROGERS, WILLIAM PIERCE (1913–). Born, Norfolk, New York; A.B., Colgate University, 1934; LL.B., Cornell University, 1937; admitted, New York bar, 1937; assistant district attorney, New York County, 1938–42, 1946–47; counsel, US Senate Special Committee to Investigate the National Defense Program, 1947; chief counsel, 1947–48; chief counsel, US Senate investigations subcommittee of Executive Expenditures Committee, 1948–50; partner, Dwight, Royall, Harris, Koegel & Caskey, New York City and Washington, D.C., 1950–53; deputy attorney general, US Department of Justice, 1953–57; attorney general, 1957–61; senior partner, Royall, Koegel, Rogers & Wells, 1961–68; secretary, US Department of State, 1969–73; presently practices law in firm of Rogers & Wells, New York City; member, several national and international committees; USNR, 1942–46. (See also *Current Biography: September 1969*.)

STEWART, POTTER (1915–   ). Born, Jackson, Michigan; B.A., cum laude, Yale University, 1937; LL.B., cum laude, 1941; fellow, Cambridge University, 1937–38; admitted, Ohio bar, 1941; New York bar, 1942; private law practice, New York City, 1941–42, 1945–47; Cincinnati, Ohio, 1947–52; member, Cincinnati City Council, 1950–53; vice-mayor, 1952–53; judge, US Court of Appeals for the Sixth Circuit, 1954–58; associate justice, US Supreme Court, 1958–   ; USNR, 1942–45; member, Phi Beta Kappa, Delta Kappa Epsilon, Phi Delta Phi, Order of the Coif. (See also *Current Biography: December 1959*.)

TROTTER, VIRGINIA YARP (1921–   ). Born, Boise, Idaho; B.S., Kansas State University, 1943; M.S., 1948; Ph.D., Ohio State University, 1960; instructor, University of Utah, 1948–50; assistant professor, head, Department of Family Economics, associate dean, College of Agriculture and Home Economics, University of Nebraska, 1950–55; director, School of Home Economics, 1963–70; dean, College of Agriculture and Home Economics, and associate director, Agricultural Experiment Station and Agricultural Extension Service, 1970–74; assistant secretary for education, US Department of Health, Education, and Welfare, 1974–   ; author, articles in professional journals.

CUMULATIVE AUTHOR INDEX

1970-1971—1974-1975

A cumulative author index to the volumes of Representative American Speeches for the years 1937-1938 through 1959-1960 appears in the 1959-1960 volume and for the years 1960-1961 through 1969-1970 in the 1969-1970 volume.

Abzug, B. S. 1971-72, 37-48, A new kind of southern strategy

Aiken, G. D. 1973-74, 66, Either impeach . . . or get off his back

Andrus, C. D. 1970-71, 137-41, The inaugural address

Barger, R. N. 1973-74, 177, Theology and amnesty

Brewster, Kingman, Jr. 1972-73, 176-93, The decade of shortcuts

Brooke, E. W. 1973-74, 74, Responsibilities inherent in a constitutional democracy

Burger, W. E. 1970-71, 13-28, State of the judiciary

Burke, Y. B. 1974-75, 143-7, "Aspirations . . . unrequited"

Butz, E. L. 1974-75, 81-8, Feast or famine: the key to peace

Carter, Jimmy, 1970-71, 142-6, Inauguration address

Cheek, J. E. 1970-71, 131-5, A promise made, a promise to keep: Whitney Young and the nation

Chisholm, Shirley. 1971-72, 27-36, Economic injustice in America today; 1972-73, 79-85, Women in politics

Church, Frank, 1970-71, 49-62, Foreign policy and the generation gap

Clifford, C. M. 1972-73, 109-18, "We must renew our confidence"

Cole, E. N. 1971-72, 93-9, Two myths and a paradox

Cox, Archibald. 1973-74, 49, Creativity in law and government

Dabney, Virginius. 1974-75, 168-80, Facts and the Founding Fathers

Dennis, D. W. 1974-75, 35-42, Hearings on articles of impeachment by the Committee on the Judiciary of the House of Representatives: for the defense

Dubos, R. J. 1972-73, 149-60, Humanizing the earth

Edwards, George. 1971-72, 101-10, Murder and gun control

Eilberg, Joshua. 1974-75, 25-9, Hearings on articles of impeachment by the Commit-

Eilberg, Joshua (*cont.*)
tee on the Judiciary of the
House of Representatives:
for the prosecution
Elson, E. L. R. 1971-72, 151-60,
Freaks for Jesus' sake

Fawcett, N. G. 1970-71, 106-14,
Direction for destiny
Flowers, Walter. 1974-75, 30-4,
Hearings on articles of im-
peachment by the Commit-
tee on the Judiciary of the
House of Representatives:
undecided
Ford, G. R. 1973-74, 193, Accep-
tance speech; 1974-75, 50-3,
First presidential address
Fulbright, J. W. 1974-75, 109-
16, "The neglect of the song"

Gallagher, Wes. 1973-74, 132,
"Free just free"
Gardner, J. W. 1972-73, 119-31,
Education; 1974-75, 158-67,
People power
Goodman, S. J. 1973-74, 160,
Raising the fallen image of
business

Harris, J. G. 1971-72, 143-50,
The prayer amendment
Hartzog, G. B., Jr. 1972-73, 194-
9, Finding America
Hatfield, M. O. 1972-73, 91-3,
Reconciliation and peace;
1973-74, 105, The energy crisis; 1974-75, 89-96, Global
interdependence: "Life, liberty, and the pursuit of happiness" in today's world
Hesburgh, T. M. 1970-71, 85-93,
Higher education begins the
seventies
Horner, M. S. 1972-73, 184-93,

Opportunity for educational
innovation
Howard, J. A. 1970-71, 94-105,
The innovation mirage
Howe, Harold II. 1972-73, 161-
75, Public education for a
humane society
Hutchins, R. M. 1971-72, 161-
71, The institutional illusion;
1974-75, 117-26, All our institutions are in disarray

James, Daniel, Jr. 1974-75, 135-
42, "Given time we'll get it
together"
Jeffrey, R. C. 1973-74, 119,
Ethics in public discourse
Johnson, L. B. 1972-73, 138-48,
As the days dwindle down
Jordan, B. C. 1974-75, 19-24,
Hearings on articles of im-
peachment by the Commit-
tee on the Judiciary of the
House of Representatives:
an introduction
Jordan, V. E., Jr. 1971-72, 49-
58, Survival; 1972-73, 39-49,
Blacks and the Nixon Ad-
ministration: the next four
years

Keeler, W. W. 1971-72, 74-7, Inaugural address of the chief
of the Cherokees
Kennedy, E. M. 1971-72, 68-73,
La Raza and the law
Kissinger, H. A. 1973-74, 87,
Statement to the Senate Foreign Relations Committee;
1974-75, 62-80, Address before
the World Food Conference

McBath, J. H. 1974-75, 127-34,
The vital university
McGill, W. J. 1971-72, 182-97,

The public challenge and the campus response

McGovern, G. S. 1972-73, 22-38, American politics: a personal view

Mathias, C. M., Jr. 1972-73, 60-3, Truth in government

Mead, Margaret. 1973-74, 97, The planetary crisis and the challenge to scientists

Mink, P. T. 1971-72, 59-67, Seeking a link with the past

Moos, M. C. 1973-74, 148, Restoring the tidemarks of trust

Moynihan, D. P. 1970-71, 29-36, The middle of the journey

Murphy, P. V. 1970-71, 122-9, What the police expect of the citizenry

Nader, Ralph. 1971-72, 79-92, Meet the Press

Nelson, G. A. 1973-74, 188, Against the nomination of Gerald R. Ford [as Vice President]

Nixon, R. M. 1970-71, 37-48, Remarks at the White House Conference on Children; 1971-72, 13-26, State of the Union message; 1972-73, 15-21, Second inaugural address; 1972-73, 50-9, The Watergate case; 1973-74, 24, Press conference; 1974-75, 43-9, Speech of resignation

Peden, William. 1972-73, 94-100, Is Thomas Jefferson relevant?

Percy, C. H. 1973-74, 189, For the nomination of Gerald R. Ford [as Vice President]

Peterson, Martha. 1970-71, 73-84, In these present crises

Powell, L. F., Jr. 1972-73, 101-8, The eroding authority

Richardson, E. L. 1973-74, 13, Vulnerability and vigilance

Rogers, W. P. 1974-75, 54-61, A brief assessment of where we stand today

Ruckelshaus, Jill. 1972-73, 65-78, Meet the Press

Ruckelshaus, W. D. 1971-72, 125-32, The environment revolution

Rusk, Dean. 1972-73, 132-7, Eulogy of Lyndon Baines Johnson

Sargent, F. W. 1973-74, 141, The computer and civil liberties

Schlesinger, Arthur, Jr. 1971-72, 133-41. Roosevelt's place in history

Schroeder, Patricia. 1972-73, 86-9, You can do it

Spencer, S. R., Jr. 1971-72, 172-81, A call for new missionaries

Steinem, Gloria. 1972-73, 65-78, Meet the Press

Stewart, Potter. 1974-75, 97-108, Or of the press

Trotter, V. Y. 1974-75, 148-57, A shift in the balance

Von Braun, Wernher. 1971-72, 111-24, Earth benefits from space and space technology

Walker, H. B. 1970-71, 63-71, The future of the past

Watson, T. J., Jr. 1970-71, 115-21, Medical care

Weicker, L. P., Jr. 1973-74, 40, The Watergate investigation

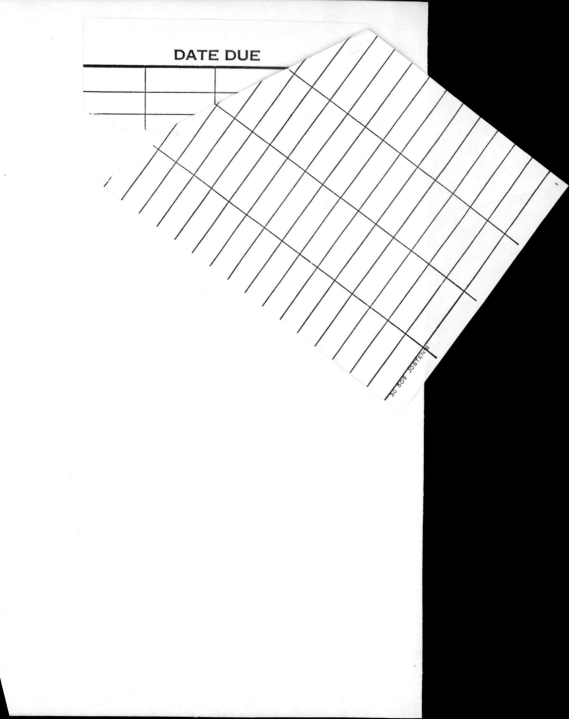

DATE DUE

30 505 JOSTENS